AF612567

Enabling People to Help Themselves

An Employment and Human Resource Development Strategy for Pakistan in the 1990's

Enabling People to Help Themselves

An Employment and Human Resource Development Strategy for Pakistan in the 1990's

John Cameron
Mohammad Irfan

ILO-ARTEP

Asian Regional Team for Employment Promotion (ARTEP)

World Employment Programme

© International Labour Organisation 1991

Publications of the International Labour Office enjoy copyright under Protocol 2 of the Universal Copyright Convention. Nevertheless, short excerpts from them may be reproduced without authorisation, on condition that the source is indicated. For rights of reproduction or translation, application should be made to the Publications Branch (Rights and Permissions), International Labour Office, CH-1211 Geneva 22, Switzerland. The International Labour Office welcomes such applications.

First published 1991

ISBN 92-2-108042-0 (Soft Cover)

ISBN 92-2-108045-5 (Hard Cover)

The designations employed in ILO publications, which are in conformity with United Nations practice, and the presentation of material therein do not imply the expression of any opinion whatsoever on the part of the International Labour Office concerning the legal status of any country, area or territory or of its authorities, or concerning the delimitation of its frontiers.

The responsibility for opinions expressed in signed articles, studies and other contributions rests solely with their authors, and publication does not constitute an endorsement by the International Labour Office of the opinions expressed in them

Reference to names of firms and commercial products and processes does not imply their endorsement by the International Labour Office, and any failure to mention a particular firm, commercial product or process is not a sign of disapproval.

Preface

The present volume is an edited version of the synthesis report on employment and human resource development strategies in Pakistan carried out under the UNDP-ILO project, "Employment and Manpower Strategies and Policies". The broader issues related to employment and human resource development of Pakistan have been presented in this study in the hope that they will be of interest to a wider audience both inside and outside Pakistan.

The volume draws upon a number of technical studies prepared under the above project. It has been prepared by Mr. John Cameron of the School of Development Studies, University of East Anglia and Mr. Mohammad Irfan of the Pakistan Institute of Development Economics, Islamabad while they were respectively the Chief Technical Advisor and the National Technical Consultant to the above UNDP-ILO project.

ILO-ARTEP wishes to thank the Government counterpart agency, Manpower Section of the Planning and Development Division of the Government of Pakistan for all the cooperation extended and the UNDP Office in Islamabad for generous financial assistance given to the project. Grateful acknowledgement is also made to the ILO Area Office, Islamabad for their help in various matters related to the completion of the work.

December 1991 ILO-ARTEP

Contents

Page

1. The Historical Background to Employment and Human Resource Development in Pakistan **1**

1.1 Development Strategies since the Creation of the State of Pakistan 1
1.2 Manpower Planning Exercises and the Five Year Plans 2
1.3 Employment Performance, Targets and Achievements 5
1.4 Employment in Agriculture 10
1.5 Non-Farm Rural Employment 12
1.6 Manufacturing Employment 13
1.7 Employment in Other Urban Sectors 15
1.8 Emigration to the Gulf Region 16
1.9 The Implications of Past Experience for Current Employment and Human Resource Development Strategy Formulation 18

2. The Challenge of Employment Creation in the 1990s **21**

2.1 The Basic Approach: A Simulation Model of an Aggregate Labour Market with Independent Labour Supply and Demand 21
2.2 The Changing Supply of People Seeking Economic Activity 24
2.3 The Changing Demands for People to Enter Employment 25
2.4 The Computer Simulation Labour Market Balances 28
2.5 Second Round Feedbacks into the Labour Market 32
2.6 Implications of the Scenario Results for Open Educated Unemployment and Poverty in Practice 36
2.7 Conclusions 39

3. Improving the Labour Market Information System **40**

3.1 The Data Needs of an Enabling Government 40
3.2 The Present Labour Market Information System 41
3.3 Clarifying Conceptualisation 44
3.4 The Project Commissioned Survey on Labour Force Measurement 47
3.5 Conclusions 56

4. The Frontiers to Employment Generation and the Need for Trading in Large Scale Units in the 1990s **58**

4.1 Introduction 58

Page

4.2 The Prospects for Employment Generation in Large Scale Agriculture and Manufacturing 59
4.3 The Public Sector and Employment Generation 67
4.4 Human Resource Skill Development as a Joint Responsibility of Government and Larger Scale Employing Units 69
4.5 Access for Women and Young People to Employment in Larger Scale Employing Units 74

5. Opportunities and Constraints with Respect to Productive Employment Creation Outside the Large Scale Employing Sector 76

5.1 Choice at the Household Level 76
5.2 The Migration Choice 79
5.3 Women's Lack of Choice 79
5.4 Patterns of Household Negative Responses to Growing Labour Market Imbalances 82
5.5 The Development Potential of Small Scale Employing Units 84

6. The Policy Framework for Enabling Productive Employment Generation in Pakistan in the 1990s 92

6.1 Background to an Enabling Strategy Formulation 92
6.2 Improved Information As a Primary Requirement 94
6.3 The Significance of Larger Scale Employing Units in Training for Human Resource Development 95
6.4 Small Scale Units as the Focus of Employment Generation 97
6.5 Improving Access to Productive Economic Activity for Women 101
6.6 An Enabling Strategy and Reducing Poverty and Contributing to Long-Run Environmental Sustainability 107
6.7 The Political Agenda 107

References 109

Annexe I 115

Annexe II 153

Index 167

List of Tables

		Page
1.1	Labour Force and Employment in (West) Pakistan 1960-61 to 1969-70	6
1.2	Gini Coefficients of Household Incomes	9
1.3	Household Income Shares	9
1.4	Person Days per Acre per Crop (Punjab)	11
1.5	Distribution of Land, 1980	12
1.6	Manufacturing Sector Annual Growth Rate (1950-86)	13
1.7	Employment Generation and Growth of Output 1961 to 1982/83	14
2.1	Simulation Model Assumption 1987-2000: Annual Growth rates by Sector	23
2.2	Quantitative Projections of Employment in the Seventh Plan	26
2.3	Employment Generation in the Seventh Plan	26
2.4	Simulation Model Results 1987-2000: Labour balance for educational level : All levels	28
2.5	Simulation Model Results 1987-2000: Labour balance for educational level: Pre-primary	29
2.6	Simulation Model Results 1987-2000: Labour balance for educational level: Primary	30
2.7	Simulation Model Results 1987-2000: Labour balance for educational level: Secondary	30
2.8	Simulation Model Results 1987-2000: Labour balance for educational level: Higher	31
3.1	Estimates of Labour Force Participation Rates 1901-1987	46
3.2	Married Female Work Participation in Pakistan by Type of Survey: 1979	47
3.3	Underemployment and Job Dissatisfaction as Estimated by the National Manpower Commission (1974-87)	47
3.4	Labour Force Participation Rate by Sex (Age 10+) by Reference Period and Measure of Labour Supply - 1989	48
3.5	Labour Force Participation Rate by Sex/ Reference Period and Measure of Labour Supply	49
3.6	Additional Unemployment due to Probing of Available for work	50

		Page
3.7	Percentage Distribution of those Available for Work by most distant place at which Available	51
3.8	Female Labour Force Participation	52
3.9	Distribution of Hours and Days Economically Active	53
3.10	Percentage Distribution of Time Utilised and Unutilised in Rural Areas by Sex	54
3.11	Job Preference of the Unemployed by Sex/Education	55
3.12	Unpaid Family Workers (Matric and above) by Level of Job Satisfaction by Rural/ Urban	56
4.1	Estimated Changes in Labour Absorption in Crop Production during 1988-2000	59
4.2	Estimated Landlessness 1980	62
4.3	Ratio of the Small Scale Sector Wage Rate to the Large Scale Sector Wage Rate 1980	63
4.4	Reasons for Installation of New Machinery	64
4.5	Compound Annual Rates of Growth of the Value Added Index, the Aggregate Input Index, and the Total Factor Productivity Index for Large Scale Manufacturing 1955-1981	65
4.6	Number of Firms Using Irregular/Contract Workers	66
4.7	Average Income of Irregular/Contract Workers by Industry	67
4.8	Civil Servants in Pakistan	68
4.9	Public Employment—Average Annual Growth Rate (1983-88)	69
4.10	Number and Enrolment in Education Institutions by Kind in Pakistan 1988-89	70
4.11	Supply of Skilled Workers, 1989	70
4.12	Supply of Semi-Skilled Workers, 1989	71
4.13	Annual Requirement of Skilled Workers and Output of Training Institutions in 1984	72
4.14	Summary of Seventh Plan Allocations for Various Sub-Sectors of Education	73
4.15	Female Representation by Occupation Based on 1973 HED Survey and 1981 Census	74
5.1	Serious Crime Statistics, 1971-89	84
5.2	(A) Composition of Rural and Urban Small Scale Industries 1983/84	86
5.2	(B) Comparison of Rural and Urban Small Manufacturing Establishments 1983/84	87
5.3	Urban and Rural Wages in Small-Scale Manufacturing, 1983/84	89

Annexed Tables

Annex I:	Project Rural Small Scale Industry Survey	115
Annex II:	Project Urban Small Scale Industry Survey	153

CHAPTER 1

The Historical Background to Employment and Human Resource Development in Pakistan

1.1 Development Strategies Since the Creation of the State of Pakistan

The development process in any society is an outcome of a historical process in which physical environments modified by human action, asset ownership patterns, cultural systems, and political/administrative structures interact with economic production, trading, and consumption opportunities.

Strategic state planners have to decide at each point in time which of these factors are "exogenous or "given" for planning purposes. From the time when the State of Pakistan was created in 1947 until the end of the 1970s (see Ahmed and Amjad 1989 for an overview), there was a period of general planning "optimism", when the "givens" were regarded as few or weak. Technology could change the physical environment, legislation could change ownership patterns, education could change cultural systems, political will could change political/administrative structures.

The 1980s, by contrast, were a decade of planning "pessimism", when the failures of state planning were totally exposed and blind following of market forces as the principal motor of "development" was accepted or imposed on all governments, with the paradoxical exception of the United States of America, on a global scale. But the decade's dominant ideology also brought with it a firmer confidence in people as active planners in their own interests than had previously existed in discussions of development. The 1990s offer an opportunity to learn from the whole post-1947 experience; to replace planning "optimism" and planning "pessimism" with planning "realism" and to redefine the principle of state planning as being to enable people's planning, rather than imposing a false dichotomy of either state planning or people's planning.

Before 1947, the area which became Pakistan produced raw materials and provided markets for industries located in British-ruled India and abroad. With the break-up of this *de facto* customs union, a considerable domestic market for consumer goods emerged together with availability of industrial raw materials and the state planners responded with a pro-industrialisation policy. This was an obvious response, in view of the ideological perceptions of the Pakistani decision makers and the international prevailing perceptions regarding the process of economic development.

To achieve industrialisation, the Pakistani planners initially stressed the encouragement of protected private entrepreneurship for the task of industrial development of the economy. Underpinned by "infant industry" arguments, various policies and measures were selected to provide an enclave for nascent large scale industrialisation. Tariff protection, an over-valued exchange rate and licensing procedures, all tended to favour a small number of entrepreneurs in large scale manufacturing. Thus a very high growth rate in the large scale manufacturing sector over a small base inherited at the time of independence was achieved during the 1950s. In addition, significant investment was made in infrastructure and public sector outlays during the decade in large-scale irrigation, hydro-electric generation, road construction and land colonisation building on previous efforts in harnessing the immense potential of the Indus basin.

Agriculture, however, stagnated because of economic and social factors such as adverse terms of trade and absence of ownership rationalisation in the interest of higher production. And being the major sector of the economy, its poor performance was reflected in low growth of the overall economy during the 1950s.

The conjunction of many favourable factors led to a significant improvement in economic performance as indicated by GDP and per capita income growth rates of the 1960s. Agricultural growth, stimulated by the installation of tubewells at a rapid rate, and by the new seed and fertiliser technology, made a major departure from the low rates of the previous decade, despite industrialisation continuing to enjoy a high level of state patronage.

Growing foreign aid and exports permitted a liberal import policy. Moreover, a de facto devaluation of the exchange rate through bonus voucher schemes in the wake of encouraging international demand for labour-intensive products, helped manufactured products enter the export market. The significant performance of these two major sectors of the economy during the 1960s resulted in an average real per capita annual growth rate of four per cent in contrast to less than one per cent during the 1950s.

But this growth performance of the 1960s was accompanied by some undesirable consequences for a long-term sustainable development of the economy. Deep socio-graphic and geographic inequalities, over-expansion of consumer goods industries at the cost of intermediate and capital goods industries, and consumption liberalisation were major inheritances from this decade of economic growth. In 1971 the new Pakistan (after the creation of Bangladesh) experienced some changes in development strategy. In order to break the hold of a few monopoly houses on industrial and financial assets, nationalisation of banks and some industries was carried out. Imbalance in the industrial structure of the economy was attempted to be rectified by establishing an intermediate and capital goods industry in the public sector. New labour and wage policies were introduced to protect the living standards of the workers.

However, the growth performance under the modified strategy during 1970-77 was not very encouraging. Natural adversities like alternating years of floods and droughts adversely affected agriculture. The international economic disorders and oil price hikes had an unfavourable impact on Pakistan's oil-importing, unevenly open economy. Public sector investment being mostly in capital-intensive projects with considerable maturity periods did not yield dividends immediately. The deterioration in international terms of trade, decline in real aid inflow and increase in debt repayments compounded the problem. All these factors combined to force the economy back to stagnation.

Parallel with a change in regime in 1977, Pakistan again entered a period of relatively rapid growth. Major factors responsible for the growth were good weather conditions for agriculture and a substantial exodus of labour to the Gulf region, which not only eased pressure on the domestic labour market but also involved significant amounts of "hard currency" remittances. Improvement in the international aid climate for Pakistan and maturing heavy industrial investments made in the early 1970s also contributed to increased real economic growth in the 1980s, which was averaging around three per cent per annum.

Formal state planning has been a continuing feature of the period since 1947, though with mixed fortunes. Economic planning was initiated in 1955-60. During 1955-70, three Five Year Plans were implemented with varying degrees of success. The Fourth Five Year Plan was formulated for the period 1970-75, but due to external and international pressures it was *de facto* abandoned. Consequently the 1970-77 period has been characterised as a non-plan period, but, even in this period, annual plans were relied upon to meet rapidly changing circumstances.

Beginning again in 1978, five year plans were formulated, and between 1978 and 1988, the Fifth and Sixth Five Year Plans were implemented. A Seventh Five Year Plan (1988-93) and also a perspective plan (1988-2003) are in existence at the start of the 1990s, though their precise implementation status given the radical political changes in 1988 is unclear.

1.2 Manpower Planning Exercises and the Five Year Plans

The First Five Year Plan contained estimates of labour force, employment and unemployment for the base year (1955). These estimates were based on the 1951 Census and Manpower Surveys.

For the plan period it was assumed that employment would increase sufficiently to absorb the incremental labour force. In contrast to its explicit objective "to increase the employment opportunities for useful employment in the country" the First Five Year Plan did not have a comprehensive approach for the assessment of manpower availability and requirement.

The Second Five Year Plan provided rough estimates of the labour force for the plan period but did not quantify future employment and unemployment. For a few selected categories of manpower supply and demand were worked out which revealed possible shortages. Accordingly, the plan stressed mobilisation and training of manpower.

The Third Five Year Plan, formulated in the context of a Perspective Plan, detailed labour force projections for 1965-85. For the plan period (1965-70), a sectoral breakdown of employed labour force was provided. In addition, the requirements of the country in six broad groups of occupation and four categories of education were estimated. These exercises were carried out by using data from other countries at a comparable stage of development. These projections implied a good deal of optimism: unemployment was to decrease from 20 per cent of the labour force to 15 per cent during the plan period. Moreover, plan figures of employment and unemployment being in man years rather than in numbers involved arbitrary conversion ratios between the plan estimates and available statistics, which served to obscure actual objectives.

The Fourth Five Year Plan provided estimates of labour force, employment and unemployment both for the beginning and the terminal year of the plan. These estimates were based on a rigorous exercise carried out by Kare Ruud and Karwanski (Ruud 1970). Using Sabolo's econometric model based on a cross country regression analysis of 40 developed and developing countries Ruud estimated manpower requirement in terms of educational levels.

There were two major weaknesses of this approach. Firstly, to the extent structural transformation of Pakistan's economy failed to conform to the average of these countries, the relevance of these projections are seriously impaired. Secondly, the sectoral productivity growth implied by these exercises were hardly plausible.

In addition to Ruud's projections, there were a few other exercises during the early 70s. Investment Advisory Centre of Pakistan and Irfan projected manpower availability and requirement for the period extending to 1985. IACP's labour requirement projections were based on assumptions such as shrinking share of agriculture in GNP as well as employment. For the manufacturing sector estimated cost per job was used to convert investment outlay into required labour.

Employment growth in other sectors was based on the rate of urbanisation and past employment growth. Irfan used the employment elasticities observed during 1963-72 to determine the labour requirement. While the availability of labour force was arrived at by using the five year average (1968-72) of the labour force participation rate.

Wilson's labour force and sectoral employment projections formed the basis of the Fifth Five Year Plan (Wilson undated). These were based on past productivity growth rates and plan targets. In addition, the Manpower Division prepared estimates of availability and requirement of 105 occupations for the plan period. The data for this latter exercise are mostly based on Annual Establishment Enquiries and few special surveys. These projections on the supply side ignored drop outs from the school and used desirable level of education for a given occupation on the demand side. Under a Pak/Netherlands project, an exercise aimed at working out the occupational and educational manpower requirement was conducted which improved upon the earlier manpower estimates.

For the Sixth Five Year Plan period two exercises were conducted. ILO's Asian Regional Team for Employment Promotion (ILO-ARTEP) worked out the requirement estimates on the basis of past employment elasticity while labour supply was arrived at by age specific labour force participation rates of 1970-80.

Cohen used an employment elasticity assumed to decline at the rate of 11 per cent on the demand side. Plan objectives on the labour supply side to increase school enrollment ratios were also incorporated.

The Manpower Division has also issued a Manpower Plan corresponding to the investment programme of the Sixth Plan. By taking into consideration the estimated labour force by major occupation groups and education in 1983, the Plan came up with requirements and supply of labour force. Adjusting for emigration, the plan identified the problems of the shortages and the surpluses.

Employment and manpower projections for the Sixth Plan were also made in another study by Kemal and Irfan for ILO-ARTEP (Irfan and Kemal 1983). This study showed slightly higher manpower requirements than the estimates of ILO-ARTEP. The main conclusion of the studies conducted by ILO-ARTEP at the request of the Planning Commission was that the employment problem was real and serious, and being compounded by return migration.

Sensitivity of the results to definitions, estimation procedures and underlying assumptions forced by a limited data base are among some of the major reasons for the imprecision of the estimates. Ideally, the labour requirement can be determined if the future sectoral investment outlay alongwith the mix of scales of production units and nature of technology is known. In order to have a fair idea about the forthcoming labour supply knowledge regarding individuals' labour market participation decisions is essential. A micro-economic behavioural perspective has been missing in the past.

1.3 Employment Performance, Targets and Achievements

Thus, specific employment planning has enjoyed even more mixed fortunes than overall state planning. The perception of the policy makers, the availability of information and date, and the nature of analytical skills available at the time of plan formulation influenced the quantification and the level of disaggregation of employment and human resource development targets in the plan documents. Gauging actual performance is equally difficult due to these data problems.

At the time of the finalisation of the First Five Year Plan (1955-60), open unemployment was not regarded as a major problem. An ILO survey in 1955 found that 2.7 per cent of the labour force was unemployed (actually looking for a job), and around 4.7 per cent of the labour force worked less than 25 hours a week. The plan document, however, preferred not to opt for a specific employment target but rather incremental labour absorption.

Non-availability of data and non-comparability among the available data sources do not permit a precise estimate of employment generation during the plan period. The evidence for the then Pakistan (inclusive of East Pakistan, currently Bangladesh) does indicate a failure of the plan to achieve the employment targets. The Second Five Year plan document, for instance, suggests that during the 1950s less than 70 per cent of the incremental labour force was absorbed by the First Five Year development programme.

Thus, the quantity of unemployment and under-employment had probably increased from 5.6 million man-years in 1951 to 7.6 million in 1961. Similarly, one estimate of underemployment, including unemployment, suggested a rise from 15 per cent in 1950 to 22 per cent of the labour force in 1960.

The Second Five Year Plan did not provide a specific employment target but provision of job opportunities to the new entrants in the labour force was an objective of the plan. The plan seriously under-estimated the growth of population and labour supply.

The Third Five Year Plan (1965-70) started from the belief that 20 per cent of the labour force was either unemployed or under-employed. The plan envisaged the creation of 2.5 million job opportunities which would outstrip the estimated 1.6 million addition to the labour force, thereby decreasing the backlog of unemployed and under-employed by about one million. Employment generation met with limited success. The estimated employment increase was only 1.28 million in contrast to the target of 2.5 million.

A major shortfall occurred in agriculture whose employment increased by 0.33 million as compared with the target of 1.14 million. Large-scale manufacturing also failed to live up to the plan's expectations. It was estimated to have created only 35 thousand jobs against the plan's anticipation of 255 thousand jobs. A host of factors such as low absorptive capacity of the industrial sector, and non-realisation of the anticipated benefits of the Green Revolution were believed to lie underneath this performance. It must be noted that this plan also under-estimated the increase in labour supply during the plan period.

But even though the plans during the 1960s (Second and Third plans) failed to achieve their targets fully, the statistics suggest that employment and under-employment actually declined as depicted in Table 1.1, suggesting that people were "planning" their own employment independently and invisibly from the state.

TABLE 1.1

Labour Force and Employment in (West) Pakistan 1960-61 to 1969-70

(million man-years)

	1960-61	1964-65	1969-70
Total Labour Force	14.27	15.46	17.55
(a) Agriculture	8.55 (59.9)	8.75 (56.6)	9.34 (53.2)
(b) Non-agriculture	5.72 (40.1)	6.71 (43.4)	8.21 (46.8)
Total Employment	12.00	13.18	16.47
(a) Agriculture	6.56	6.72	8.51
(b) Manufacturing	1.84	2.24	2.48
(c) Others	3.60	4.22	5.48
Unemployment			
(a) Agriculture	1.99 (23.3)	1.13 (12.9)	0.83 (8.9)
(b) Non-Agriculture	0.28 (4.9)	0.25 (3.7)	0.25 (3.0)

Source Naseem 1981

During 1970-77, as already discussed, the practice of Five Year Plan formulations could not be continued. It was during this period that, for the first time in the history of Pakistan, unemployment was perceived as a major problem. The governmental responses to the problem were through crash programmes and through increasing recruitment to the ranks of the services and public enterprises. This led to a decline in unemployment particularly among the educated youth. However, given the overall low growth of the economy, the employment increase has been achieved at the cost of decreasing labour productivity. For instance, employment in agriculture grew by 16 per cent during 1970-77 while the output growth was 11.4 per cent for the same period.

The Fifth Plan (1978-83) was formulated in a substantially changed environment as labour migration to the Gulf region was already taking the edge off the unemployment problem of the country. The Fifth Plan relied on growth in agriculture, rural development and social sectors to take major responsibility for job creation. The employment targets of the plan were to create jobs not only for the additional levels of unemployment and under-employment but to reduce the backlog of unemployment. The Sixth Five Year Plan had a targeted increase in employment opportunities of 3.32 million during the period 1983-88. The employment growth was expected to be 2.4 per cent annum during the plan period. A perusal of the two labour force surveys of 1982-83 and 1967-87 suggests that employment in fact registered a high rate of growth of 2.6 per cent and was likely to exceed the plan target. This achievement on the labour-use side was more than offset by a rise of labour supply greater than anticipated.

Population growth turned out to be 3.06 per cent per annum instead of 2.85 per cent as in the plan and instead of the expectation of net outmigration of 0.55 million people, there had been a net reverse migration of June 1978. Hence, there may have been some deterioration in the unemployment and underemployment situation of the country.

Notwithstanding the ostensible inclusion of employment objectives in the various plan documents, the articulation of these objectives into a set of well-defined policy measures left much to be desired. Insofar as the process of development has resulted in growing employment at about the rate needed to employ a growing labour force, this seems to have been largely independent of formal state planning.

In general, employment and human resource development goals were not prioritised in the overall objectives of the various five years plans as the formulation of major sectoral strategies was primarily governed by production targets. The educational and skill development programmes of the country took their own course mostly in isolation from the developments taking place elsewhere in the economy, especially from the changing demand pattern of the economy. Integration of issues related to labour use and co-ordination amongst the various sectors of the economy was hardly attempted in the various plan documents. Worst of all, the supply side pressures generated by the demographic processes continued to be underestimated.

Employment promotion as such never received the treatment befitting a primary objective of the planning efforts. Not only was it an appendix in the framework of planning but generally an afterthought addition to the growth targets in GNP. Employment and human resource development may be considered to have been technically included in the planning process but subjected to changing modes of analysis yielding inaccurate predictions. These changes and inaccuracies may have been both causes and effects given formal planning's tendency to neglect employment and human resource development.

That such inaccuracy and neglect did not prove too costly in terms of the emergence of massive unemployment is due to a variety of domestic and external factors. The independence of the country in 1947 brought in its wake large numbers of job opportunities associated with moves up the administrative structure and the development of social infrastructure for a sovereign state, relative to the small number of educated. Thus until the late 1960s, unemployment, particularly among the politically sensitive group of educated urban youth, did not rise to disturbing levels.

Around the close of the decade of 1960s, with the reduction in foreign aid inflow, the decline in investment/GDP ratio, and the resultant stagnation in the growth of the non- agriculture sector, the problem of unemployment, particularly among the educated youth, made its appearance. Disgruntled and jobless youth expressed their disapproval through an unprecedented level of riots in the country. According to the Housing Economic and Demographic Survey of 1973, one-third of the unemployed had at least primary education. Slightly half of these were graduates of high schools or higher institutions. Over 42 thousand of the unemployed had college or university education.

The response of the government was to increase employment in the public sector enterprises and other crash programmes like the People Works Programme and the National Development Volunteer Programme. These measures were more or less short-term palliatives but they generated considerable job opportunities, although it is difficult to quantify them. The efficacy, sufficiency and sustainability of these programmes would have been questioned had they not been overshadowed by the boom in labour migration to the Gulf region.

The Gulf region boom led to sizeable emigration of Pakistani workers, to the tune of 2 to 2.5 million during the 1975-82 period. In other words, during this period roughly 25 per cent of the incremental labour force moved out of the country, which for a while actually caused a shortage of labour. The pressure to lay a foundation for the development of the economy consistent with needed job opportunities was relieved. In fact, some of the consequent policies bearing upon relieving apparent shortages of labour in various productive sectors such as raising the level of mechanisation in agriculture turned out to be counter-productive and inconsistent with the basic factor endowment and long-terms needs of the economy.

More recently with the end of net out-migration and the onset of return migration the problem of unemployment has re-emerged. The precise quantification of unemployment is yet to be made, as the data provided by Labour Force Surveys have been considered inadequate to reflect the true level of the unemployment and its concentration among politically sensitive groups.

But the issue of employment and human resource development cannot be reduced to fluctuations in unemployment among politically sensitive groups. For instance, a significant level of overall income inequality has remained stubbornly unchanged over decades (see Tables 1.2 and 1.3). To understand the processes by which the mass of the Pakistani people (which still means rural and illiterate in

1990) have found ways to earn incomes in changing circumstances requires a sectoral analysis which must start with agriculture.

TABLE 1.2

Gini Coefficients of Household Incomes

(1.00 = Perfect Equality)

	Pakistan	Rural	Urban
1963-64	0.39	0.36	0.44
1966-67	0.36	0.33	0.39
1969-70	0.34	0.30	0.37
1970-71	0.33	0.30	0.37
1971-72	0.35	0.31	0.38
1979	0.37	0.32	0.39
1984-85	0.39	0.34	0.40

Source: Statistics Division for 1979 and 1984-85; *Economic Survey, 1986-87*, Economic Advisor's Wing, Ministry of Finance, for the rest; in *Seventh Five Year Plan, 1988-93*, Planning Commission, Government of Pakistan, undated.

TABLE 1.3

Household Income Shares

(% of Total)

	Lowest		Highest	
	20%	40%	20%	10%
Pakistan				
1970-71	8.2	20.5	41.4	26.8
1979	7.4	18.8	45.5	31.0
1984-85	6.9	17.9	46.7	32.1
Rural				
1970-71	8.7	21.6	38.8	24.1
1979	8.3	20.9	41.3	27.1
1984-85	7.7	19.7	42.8	28.4
Urban				
1970-71	7.5	18.9	45.1	30.6
1979	6.9	17.8	47.0	32.2
1984-85	6.8	17.4	47.7	32.8

Source: Federal Bureau of Statistics for 1979 and 1984-85; Pakistan Institute of Development Economics for 1970-71; in *Seventh Five Year Plan 1988-93*, Planning Commission, Government of Pakistan, undated.

1.4 Employment in Agriculture

Given that the majority of the workforce still find employment in agriculture in 1990, the secular decline in the labour absorptive capacity of agriculture has created a continuing pressure on other sectors to generate disproportionate amounts of employment. Declining labour absorption has to some extent resulted from various forces generated by the policy environment, the technological choices and skewed land distribution which provided a structural bias for labour displacing technological developments.

The agriculture sector experienced a virtual stagnation during the decade of 1950s primarily because of policy neglect and insufficient irrigation water. During the next decade (1960-70), agriculture displayed a commendable performance by registering 5 per cent annual growth in contrast to 1.7 per cent for the previous decade. This was mostly due to increased water through the installation of tube-wells in the years of the decade. The introduction of high yielding varieties, and increased application of fertiliser around 1966 further spurred this growth process. During the four years of 1966-70, the output index increased by 46 per cent.

But agriculture experienced stagnation again due to bad weather during the first half of 1970s. Its production index hardly increased from what was realised in 1969-70. During the second half of the decade, agricultural production staged a recovery and since then the pace of growth remained respectable. During the Sixth Five Year Plan (1983-88), agricultural output has been estimated to have grown at around four per cent per annum.

Initial phases of agricultural output growth during the early 1960s were characterised by labour augmenting technological development such as extended irrigation facilities, increasing application of fertiliser and introduction of high yield varieties such as Maxi Pak Wheat. But during the late 1960s, tractors were introduced in considerable numbers.

The impact of tractorisation on labour use in agriculture has been the subject of many studies. A number of studies have clearly shown the labour displacement effect of tractors. However, other studies, particularly those conducted in the late 1960s and 1970s, have also argued that the direct labour displacement effect has been more than counter-balanced by the indirect output increasing effect of tractors. More recently, a survey comparing 1976/77 and 1983/84 found that total labour use per cultivated hectare declined during this period by about six per cent. Government policy regarding mechanisation, particularly the introduction of tractors, was initially based on the consideration that in a country of small holdings with abundant labour, rapid mechanisation should not be encouraged. This policy, reflected in various documents (from the Royal Commission Report of 1928 to the Inquiry Committee Report of 1952), had undergone a change by 1960 when tractorisation was seen as both output and employment increasing (Hussain,1988,105). Policy perception does not appear to have significantly changed since then.

Various supportive policies engendered an incentive network leading to a tremendous increase in the tractors. Agricultural machinery, particularly tractors, enjoyed favourable purchasing terms even in comparison with industrial machinery. In contrast to a 40 per cent import duty on machinery, the assembled large tractors and their components were subject to only 10 per cent import duty during the 1970s. Cheap credit policies played their role too. In fact, the real interest rate on medium and long-term advances from the Agricultural Development Bank of Pakistan (ADBP) during 1973-77 was negative.

TABLE 1.4

Person Days Per Acre Per Crop (Punjab)

Specification	Wheat	Cotton	Maize	Grains
All bullock	27	38	38	18
Mechanical cultivate only	25	35	32	14
Mechanical cultivate & threshing	21	35	32	14
Mechanical cultivate, threshing & cartage	19	29	29	13
Mechanical cultivate, threshing, cartage and harvest	14	18	—	—

Source: Irfan 1989.

It must be noted that according to some estimates three- quarters of private tractors were financed by ADBP loans. Furthermore, cheap diesel prices lowered the operational costs of the tractors.

Thus it can be seen that policy environments actively encouraged mechanisation in agriculture, which led to curtailment in labour use. The use of these modern inputs exerted pressure to enlarge operational holdings. Land concentration among larger farm sizes and tractorisation are indeed pushing Pakistan's agriculture along the path of commercialisation.

The importance of farm size distribution for employment generation in agriculture can hardly be over-emphasised. Farm size defined as both the scale of operation and form of organisation tends to influence the factor mix cropping pattern and intensity. The conditions of labour use such as wage versus kind payment, permanent versus casual labour and use of family labour instead of hired labour tend to vary across different farm sizes. It must be noted, however, that distribution itself can be effected by policies such as land reform, availability of technological options and supporting policies, but these policies themselves take account of the interests of the large farm lobby with its own agenda of profitability and labour control.

Pakistan introduced land reforms thrice in 1959, 1972 and 1977. Legally there has been a gradual decline in the permissible ceiling on ownership. But of the total cultivated area, only 9.2 per cent was distributed among 178 thousand persons under these three land reforms. In general, rural inequality grew between 1960 and 1980 as shown in Tables 1.2 and 1.3. Table 1.5 shows one indicator of inequality in control of land in 1980.

Table 1.5 shows that the largest 10 percent of farmers were reported as cultivating over one-third of the total land area in Pakistan in the Agricultural Census of 1980. Processes exist that tend to concentrate land-holding among large farm sizes alongside a decline in tenant farms' numbers and areas. A perusal of the Agricultural Censuses of 1972 and 1980 suggests a decline in labour use per unit area, particularly among large farm sizes.

TABLE 1.5

Land Distribution 1980

Size of Farm (acres)	Per cent of farms	Per cent of cultivated area
Under 0.5	8	0
0.5 to under 1.0	9	2
1.0 to under 2.0	17	6
2.0 to under 3.0	17	9
3.0 to under 5.0	23	21
5.0 to under 10.0	17	26
10.0 to under 20.0	6	17
20.0 to under 60.0	3	13
Above 60.0	<1	6

Source: Pakistan Economic Survey, 1988-89.

A declining labour absorptive capacity in agriculture has also involved a substitution of family and casual labour for permanently hired labour. In addition, the labour : land ratio in the medium and large farms appears to have declined during the 1972-80 period.

1.5 Non-farm Rural Employment

The agrarian transition experienced by Pakistan as discussed in the preceding section was characterised by declining labour use per unit of land. This forced the landless rural labour force to look for productive employment elsewhere both in rural and urban areas as well as in other countries. Rural to urban migration and temporary international emigration, particularly to the Gulf region have been some of the responses of the rural population to the problem of decreasing agricultural employment availability.

Equally important has been the growth of employment opportunities in the rural non-farm sector which demonstrated a higher rate of employment growth than agriculture during 1971-81 period. The diversity of these activities together with limited information make it difficult to reach meaningful, precise conclusions on actual numbers or productivity of jobs created. Broadly speaking, there appear to be three major sources of the growth in these activities.

Firstly, the nature and level of growth in the farm sector has developed input and product market interdependence between farm and non-farm sector. For instance, tubewell introduction in agriculture during the early 1960s has been regarded as a positive force in the development of simple tool manufacturing and repair work-shops in the rural areas.

Secondly, the non-farm sector has been experiencing growth due to expansion of state services in the country. Over time, increase in educational and health institutions has generated a significant number of job opportunities in rural areas.

Thirdly, various rural development programmes under different names have been introduced in Pakistan. Employment generation has been one of the objectives in these programmes. No serious attempt has been made to estimate the quantum of job creation under these rural development programmes. That all these programmes met with limited success appears to be the major conclusion of a few studies undertaken in the past. These programmes, being paternalistic in spirit, failed to enlist the participation of the planned beneficiaries. The local bodies had little powers and bureaucratic controls were alleged to be responsible for the limited success in transforming the rural areas for self-sustained long-term development.

Rural, small-scale non-farm employment has not been well documented in Pakistan and we make recommendations to improve the data base, but a recent survey is reported in Section 5.5 (and associated annexed Tables), and the sector is strongly supported for development in Chapter 6.

1.6 Manufacturing Employment

Rapid industrialisation has remained one of the major policy objectives in Pakistan. Only a very modest base was inherited at the time of independence, and the manufacturing sector registered an impressive growth of eight per cent per annum over the 1950-86 period in real value-added. The growth rates had been substantially higher during the first two decades (1950-70) than during 1970-80. For the last six years of the 1980s, the growth rate over an expanded base has again risen to the level of the first two post-independence decades. The time profile of estimated growth rates of large and small-scale sectors is provided in Table 1.6.

TABLE 1.6

Manufacturing Sector Annual Growth Rate (1950-86)

Period	Large-scale	Small-scale	Total
1950-60	15.4	2.3	7.7
1960-70	13.3	2.9	9.9
1970-80	4.7	7.9	5.5
1980-86	9.5	9.4	9.5
1950-86	10.8	5.2	8.0

Source: Irfan 1989.

Since the manufacturing sector exhibited a higher average growth rate than GDP over time its share went up from 7.8 per cent in 1949-50 to almost 20 per cent of GDP in the late 1980s. The measured share of small-scale manufacturing in

GDP experienced a decline from 5.5 per cent in 1949 to a low of 3.5 per cent, but thereafter rose again to 5.5 per cent. The share of the large-scale manufacturing sector in GDP, by contrast, increased by seven times (2.2 per cent in 1949-50 to 14.5 per cent in 1985-86).

Governmental patronage was mostly confined to large-scale manufacturing industries, though primarily as an import substitution strategy. For the first two decades (1950-70), import substitution strategy in the consumer goods industries was mainly applied to textile and food industries. During the 1970s, an import substitution strategy was extended to intermediate and capital goods industries. However, even at present the consumer goods industries still account for a predominant share in the large-scale manufacturing output. Around two-thirds of the value-added products are still generated by the textile, food and beverages industries. Employment generation in the large-scale manufacturing sector has been less impressive than its growth in value terms. In comparison to the investment outlay and respectable growth in value added, estimated expansion in job opportunities in this sector has not been encouraging as shown in Table 1.7.

TABLE 1.7

Employment Generation and Growth of Output

(1961 to 1982/83)

	Change in Output at Constant Prices of 1956/60		Change in Employment (in millions)	
Period	Rs. Millions	%	Millions	%
1961 to 1969-70	2,756	134.2	1.03	60.2
1960-70 to 1974-75	950	18.3	0.00	0.0
1974-75 to 1978-79	1,421	23.2	0.67	24.5
1978-79 to 1982-83	3,888	51.4	0.49	14.5
1961 to 1982-83	9,015	439.0	2.19	128.1

Source. Irfan 1989.

Employment elasticity in large-scale manufacturing with respect to value of output during the period 1961-83 has been estimated to be only 0.29 and appears to have drastically declined in recent years, though, as we shall see, employment underestimation may play a significant role in these measurements.

Policies encouraging the growth of the large-scale manufacturing sector have been related to manipulating the exchange rate, fiscal incentives and import restrictions. Large-scale manufacturers purchased capital equipment and industrial raw materials at Pakistan Rupee prices much lower than those prices would have been without government policies. Simultaneously the over-valued exchange rate permitted the purchase of domestic raw materials at Rupee prices lower than those which would have been obtained at a more realistic exchange rate. Import restrictions through tariff and non-tariff barriers increased the profitability of the domestically produced import substitutes.

Furthermore, fiscal incentives of various kinds such as a 5-year tax holiday (a subsidy equivalent to one-third of capital) and under-accelerated and depreciated allowances constituted major policy instruments favouring use of imported machinery and other inputs.

The Pakistan economy became much more open and exposed with the total percentage of GDP traded rising from 10.3 per cent in 1969/70 to 27.6 per cent in 1987/88 (Kemal 1990). In both Pakistan Rupee and vital hard currency terms, there was a significant rise in the capital cost of job creation in the manufacturing sector. However, rising capital intensity during the 1970s and 1980s also partly resulted from a shift from consumer goods to heavy engineering industries and may also be a consequence of increasing underestimation of the labour force in large scale manufacturing (see Chapters 3 and 4).

Over time policy has been moving unevenly away from such blatantly discriminatory policies. The over-valued exchange rate was scaled down in 1972 when the Pakistani rupee was devalued which diminished cost disadvantages to small-scale manufacturing industries which was generally more labour-intensive and export-oriented. Small-scale industry developed at a real value-added annual growth rate (8.7 per cent) higher than large-scale (7 per cent) industry's during 1972-86. It must be noted that the cost of job creation in the large scale sector is currently believed to be 80 times that in the small-scale manufacturing sector, though we will cast doubt on this estimate later.

Using the generally accepted data, the major employment expansion in manufacturing predominantly occurred in the small or informal manufacturing sector while large-scale manufacturing exhibited a limited growth in labour use. For instance, 34.6 per cent of the manufacturing employment in 1972 was estimated to be in small or informal manufacturing, but this share rose to 65 per cent in Sind and 74 per cent in Punjab by 1984-85. However, results of a recent survey reported in Chapter 4 throw some doubts on these figures suggesting much under-reporting of large-scale manufacturing employment.

The tariff structure has undergone a change favouring capital and intermediate goods industries. It is difficult to quantify the impact of this shift in protection. To the extent that the consumer goods industry is more labour-intensive, such a policy change may lead to curtailment in labour absorption. However, the presence of strong backward and forward linkages associated with engineering and chemical industries may have a substantial impact on employment generation through linkages between large scale and small-scale units.

1.7 Employment in other Urban Sectors

At present roughly three-fourths of urban employment is believed to be provided by small-scale, unregulated or so-called informal sectors. More than 90 per cent of the employment in the trade and construction sectors is contributed by these so-called informal activities. Around three-quarters of the employment in transport and manufacturing and one-half of the employment in service sectors fall under these unregulated or small-scale activities.

During the 1980s, this sector appeared to exhibit dynamism both in growth of output as well as employment. The underlying reasons for this growth have not been well explored. There is, however, a recognition of the role of remittances from the Gulf region which added to the demand for such activities and possibly to the funds for financing such activities.

There is very little data on this sector and we may be justifiably accused of having treated it as last-resort, residual employment except insofar as it appears in urban small-scale manufacturing or women's urban employment. We would expect the recommendations we make to improve data collection, which if implemented, would allow future authors to treat this sector more sensitively.

1.8 Emigration to the Gulf Region

Emigration of Pakistani workers to the Gulf region labour market probably constitutes one of the major influences on the Pakistan economy of the past two decades. Consequent upon the economic boom in the Middle East led by the oil price hike in 1973, the Gulf region labour-short economies started recruiting workers from South and South-East Asian countries for their massive infrastructural and other developmental programmes.

This opportunity, particularly for Pakistan, to export labour at a time when the economy was beset with the problems of unemployment, stagflation and balance of payment problems, was regarded as an unquestionable boon. Not only was it seen to offer a release from the growing pressures on the domestic employment situation but it was also considered to provide an access to much needed foreign exchange.

Since 1975, there has been an outflow of workers to the Gulf region economies. However, the rising trend was arrested around 1982. After 1982, with the onset of economic recession and the phasing out of the construction boom, the intake of expatriate labour in those economies underwent a drastic curtailment and experienced a compositional change too. At present, the annual flow of workers from Pakistan to the Gulf region appears to be more or less in balance with the numbers of return migrants thereby making little or no difference to changes in the domestic labour supply.

The experience of mass labour export, though short-lived, had a tremendous impact on society, economy and in fact the whole fabric of the society. A better understanding of the issues related with this emigration fundamentally can be had only in a multi-disciplinary, multi-level framework including household decision-making.

The effects of these two related flows (labour outflow and remittances inflow) had a differential impact on different segments of the population and markets of the economy. To begin with, the flow of emigrants was uneven in terms of spatial origin. A majority of them belonged to rural areas, particularly, the northern Punjab and North West Frontier Province (NWFP) while the labour exodus from rural Sind was relatively low.

The occupational composition of Pakistani emigrants was overwhelmingly dominated by those joining the construction and transport sectors with forty percent unskilled workers. During the 1980s, at the same time as sluggish demand conditions emerged in the Gulf region, demand for all types of skills for the service sector has tended to replace that for construction workers. A shift which

Pakistan has found difficult to adjust to in terms of skill and sectoral requirements.

The dual effect of labour and remittance flows on the economy has been a subject matter of various studies. In a recent publication (Amjad 1989), the experience of various labour sending countries from the ESCAP region has been documented. There is a recognition that disentangling the influence of labour exodus on the economy from the various other forces which were operative simultaneously is a complex task. The impression lent by this set of studies is that the associations yielded by macro-level data between different variables such as the remittances or labour export or commodity export can at best be regarded as coincidental rather than interpreted as a stable macro-economic relationship and is based on millions of individual decisions made in the light of particular micro-economic circumstances.

The macro-economic impact of labour exodus and inflow of remittances depends upon: (a) importance of labour outflow and remittances in the overall economy; (b) initial conditions of the economy; (c) the governmental policies which tended to dilute or enhance the impact of labour export and use of remittances. The export of labour from a developing country to a capital-rich labour-short economy may appear to represent a mutually beneficial partial integration, confined to the labour market only, of the two economies .

In Pakistan the exodus of labour in the late 1970s and early 1980s should have been significant in reducing the growth in the total domestic labour force, and hence reducing unemployment. During 1975-82, Pakistan exported labour which amounted to around a quarter of its incremental labour force. But the unemployment rates yielded by Labour Force Surveys remained quite insensitive to this migration. Partly this may have been due to the inadequacy of the data. Part of the reason could be previously discouraged workers re-entering the labour market. An additional reason could be the changes in the factor mix and absorptive capacity of the economy partly or wholly related to labour export.

A careful examination of the wage data pertaining to Pakistan is indicative of a significant rise in the real wages of all the workers coinciding with the period of massive outflow of workers to the Gulf region. Research studies (Irfan 1983 and Irfan and Ahmad 1985) analysed these wage changes and concluded that labour export has been an influential factor in raising the real wages of the workers in the domestic labour market.

Some studies have tried to document the effect of labour exodus and wage rise on choice of the factor proportions in the economy. In a survey of construction and transport firms in 1982, it was found that wage costs as a fraction of output have risen over time implying that labour productivity in value terms has deteriorated or failed to match the growth in wages. The employers in response did appear to resort to selective mechanisation in the medium term. For instance, the construction industry reduced the share of wages directly through introduction of machines and indirectly through the use of pre-fabricated material.

Similarly, the shift towards higher capital intensity through mechanisation in agriculture could also be interpreted as a by-product of labour shortage occasioned by labour exodus. The evidence on elasticity of employment with respect to value added for various sectors of the economy tends to substantiate the claim that there has been a shift from less capital intensive to more capital intensive techniques of production during the late 1970s and early 1980s.

On the other hand, although it is difficult to assess the total impact of remittances on the economy, the evidence at the macro level hardly suggests that either the saving rate or investment as a fraction of the GDP experienced a significant rise as a consequence of the inflow of remittances. The expenditure pattern out of the remittances of the recipient households involves a major portion being spent on consumption and construction or renovation of houses. Some remittances, though a small share, are invested in financial assets.

The consumption pattern engendered by the inflow of remittances through a demonstration effect may have had adverse repercussions on the saving behaviour of the non- recipient households too. The likelihood that the remittances tend to substitute for, rather than augment, domestic savings, though not very well explored by the researchers, can hardly be ruled out.

Increased expenditure facilitated by remittances has undeniably had a bearing on the sectoral pattern of investment. One of the effects of increased expenditure due to remittances has been that the consumption pattern particularly in urban areas has shifted towards consumer durables using electricity. Purchasing ownership of dwellings also appears to have been a highly favoured sector for the first round of remittances expenditure.

Similarly, increased demand for consumer durables by remittance recipient and other households (through the demonstration effect) led to local production of a number of consumer durable products. For instance, growth in the plastics industry and engineering industry in producing appliances such as washing machines and coolers, have been notable growth sectors in manufacturing. Similarly, the construction boom had an impact on related industries such as electrical, sanitary wares and metal fixtures.

While the Gulf Region labour market is still heavily dependent upon non-national workers and the reconstruction of infrastructure in Iraq, Afghanistan, and Iran may also require foreign labour, the likelihood of recurrence of such substantial labour export as experienced during late 1970s or early 1980s hardly appears to be in the offing. At present, it would be rash to assume other than that outmigration and return migration tend to cancel each other with the result that domestic labour market will have to continue to absorb the increasing supply of labour.

1.9 The Implications of Past Experience for Employment and Human Resource Development Strategy Formulation

Until recently, Pakistan state planners have not had to develop long-term, active, direct employment or human resource development strategies or policies. The indirect impacts of other development policies or wholly external factors have combined to dampen any emerging problems in these areas. But each of these factors: staffing the state apparatus, larger-scale industrialisation, that "green revolution" in agriculture, and international migration, has left an inheritance, often with negative implications for current strategy and policy formulation and implementation.

The large state has encouraged the attitude that obtaining academic educational qualifications or contacts with politicians should guarantee secure office employment. Short term crash programmes to meet immediate crises of "educated unemployment" reinforce this attitude and have created increased problems for the future.

Large-scale industry has been built up on a basis of, and grown used to, both access to imported inputs and low cost labour. Greater exposure to international competition is likely to result in efforts to push the wage-bill down by reducing numbers employed and real wage rates. Casualisation of the large-scale industrial workforce is already well advanced as a process and serves to directly and indirectly reduce wage-bills. There must also be a concern that employers will continue to see mechanisation as a means to quality improvement and ensuring continuous production, rather than training or enlightened industrial relations.

The initial "green revolution" based on new seed and chemical inputs and irrigation resulted in increased labour use in agriculture, though this labour was still illiterate and low paid. But it seems that any hint of labour shortage has been met by mechanisation. This has also allowed profits to continue to be obtained in agriculture independent of investment in human resource development and, indeed, at some cost in overall employment. The physical and social patterns of agricultural production are based on illiterate labour working alongside machinery with employers responding to seasonal or local labour shortages with further mechanisation. There are powerful political interests which have been strengthened by past processes that see no advantage in changing these patterns.

The experience of labour export has also actually led to the creation of employment and human resource development problems. In addition to the above mentioned changes in the factor mix and consumption patterns across all sectors in Pakistan, there is a risk of governmental complacency in treating the export of the labour of unskilled workers as a continuing part of a long term solution to growing labour market imbalance. That Pakistan will enter the 1990s with very little possibility for significantly increased labour export must be incorporated in the design of a realistic employment strategy.

The combination of these processes has had profound implications for education and training in Pakistan. At no time have powerful interests been advocating state development of education and training. The state planning process for education and training has been driven by well-meaning intentions from the planners, not by imperatives from the wider society and economy. Large-scale enterprises appear to be adjusted to substituting mechanisation for training and accepting lower technical efficiency and lower quality output than the machinery could optimally produce.

On the positive side, Pakistani people have shown considerable initiative in finding ways to be economically active since 1947 despite the unpromising wider environment. The challenge, which is recognised by the National Manpower Commission, is to halt the historical processes which are working against productive employment and human resource development by large-scale employers and enable and facilitate existing and potential initiatives by millions of people seeking to be productively economically active. In recognising that meeting this challenge goes against the grain of previous history, Pakistan's state planners should recognise the need to break with past attitudes and approaches and think afresh about all the "givens" from the past.

CHAPTER 2

The Challenge of Employment Creation in the 1990s

2.1 The Basic Approach: A Simulation Model of an Aggregate Labour Market with Independent Labour Supply and Demand

In Chapter 1, it was shown how the accumulated inheritance from the past has produced a legacy which has tended to set obstacles to future employment and human resource development, and also to limit experience of government in strategic, longer-term promotion of higher productivity employment. But clearly this would be unimportant if the autonomous "people planned" development of the Pakistan economy were expected to produce sufficient employment in the 1990s.

In this chapter, likely future developments will be discussed in the time period of current perspective planning in Pakistan looking towards the year 2000. The modelling approach adopted here uses the concept of a relatively open labour market in which supply and demand for labour interact to move the market towards equilibrium. People wanting or needing paid employment are assumed to be willing and able to move locations and accept variations in rates of earnings as part of this equilibrating process.

To simulate this process, a labour market computer model for the Pakistan situation is utilised (Gulbrandsen 1990). The parameters for the model were based on population, education and labour force data sources for Pakistan in the 1980s. Fine-tuning calibration of the model brought the simulation results for 1987 into line with the actual measurements for that year. On this basis, the model was then run to simulate developments during the 1990s. The structure of the model is described in detail elsewhere (Gulbrandsen 1990). For our purposes here, only the major qualitative characteristics of the model are described.

(i) The growth in numbers of people potentially available for the labour force (the "labour pool" in the model) is determined by the whole population over 10 years of age, therefore the labour pool grows at about the same rate as overall population;

(ii) The labour pool is divided into sub-groups by four completed levels of schooling (pre-primary completion, primary completion, secondary completion, higher/tertiary completion). Movements between levels are governed by initial enrollment and standard rates of drop-out by grade year, derived with difficulty from Pakistan education statistics for the 1980s;

(iii) The labour supply, in terms of numbers of people available for work at a variety of locations at a range of rates of earnings, is calculated by applying standard Labour Force Participation Rates with respect to the labour pools for each level of schooling by gender. This calculation utilises information on measured Labour Force Participation Rates for Pakistan with respect to the whole non-student population over the age of 10 years (including the very low rate officially accorded to women) with allowance made for the presence of students in the model's "labour pool";

(iv) The labour demand side of the market is based on a rate and pattern of economic growth derived from the experience of the 1980s. This is disaggregated into nine sectors, the division of total investment between sectors and each sector's performance is simulated from actual Pakistan 1980s data (see Table 2.1);

(v) Each sector is associated with a pattern of seven types of job/occupation and a consequent pattern of demand for people with different levels of schooling. These patterns are empirically based on Labour Force Surveys and therefore contain inevitable small, statistical anomalies, such as a few "illiterate professionals";

(vi) These patterns are steadily modified over time by slowly increasing (by a percentage point or so) the amount of fixed capital per worker and the level of schooling required for each occupation. Hence labour productivity is also assumed to increase, in the simulation reported here by about three per cent per annum;

(vii) With the demand side and supply sides specified, the simulation can then be used to calculate labour balances, i.e net vacant full-time jobs or wholly unemployed people readily available for work.

The results of the simulation reported here can be taken as a "best informed" trend estimate of likely labour market performance in Pakistan in the 1990s. As a "best informed" trend estimate, the simulation is only as good as the data for the 1980s (more about which will be said in Chapter 3). When compared with the World Bank 1989 "high" and "low" estimates, the simulation reported here is closer to the "low" and may thus be considered relatively optimistic.

The unemployment results of the simulation are sensitive to small variations in some assumptions, notably the Labour Force Participation Rates out of the "labour pool". As indicated in the World Bank 1989 report, the estimated rate can increase markedly with easily justifiable upward adjustments in Labour Force Participation Rates. Estimates of unemployment rates must be treated as indicators

TABLE 2.1

Simulation Model Assumption 1987-2000
Annual Growth rates by Sector

Year	Agricul-ture	Mining	Manu-facturing	Construc-tion	Electricity	Trans-port	Commerce	Finance	Service	Total	Per capita
1988	3.1	19.3	8.9	5.2	9.5	6.3	8.2	8.3	6.9	6.3	2.7
1989	3.2	17.1	8.6	5.2	9.1	6.2	8.0	8.1	6.8	6.3	2.7
1990	3.3	15.4	8.4	5.3	8.9	6.2	7.8	7.9	6.7	6.3	2.6
1991	3.4	14.1	8.2	5.3	8.6	6.2	7.7	7.8	6.7	6.2	2.6
1992	3.5	13.1	8.0	5.3	8.4	6.2	7.5	7.6	6.6	6.2	2.6
1993	3.5	12.2	7.8	5.3	8.2	6.1	7.4	7.5	6.6	6.2	2.6
1994	3.6	11.5	7.7	5.3	8.0	6.1	7.3	7.4	6.5	6.1	2.5
1995	3.7	10.9	7.5	5.4	7.8	6.1	7.2	7.2	6.4	6.1	2.5
1996	3.7	10.4	7.4	5.4	7.6	6.0	7.1	7.1	6.4	6.1	2.4
1997	3.8	9.9	7.3	5.4	7.5	6.0	7.0	7.0	6.3	6.1	2.3
1998	3.9	9.5	7.1	5.4	7.4	6.0	6.9	6.9	6.3	6.0	2.3
1999	3.9	9.2	7.0	5.4	7.2	6.0	6.8	6.8	6.3	6.0	2.2
2000	4.0	8.9	6.9	5.4	7.1	5.9	6.7	6.8	6.2	6.0	2.2

Source: Cameron scenario of model described in Gulbrandsen, 1990.

of directions of pressures on the market (and hence on Government), not as point measures for policy fine-tuning.

After separate discussions of the supply and demand sides of the labour market, the pattern of reported unemployment rates from the simulation will be separately analysed below to reveal the direction of adjustments which market forces will produce independently of new policy action.

2.2 The Changing Supply of People Seeking Economic Activity

(a) Labour supply increases due to births in the 1980s:

The simulation model uses the results of the 1981 Population Census to derive age- and gender-specific population structures for each year. Possible anomalies in the distribution of population by age in 1981 produces variations in estimated population growth rates which will need to be updated by the 1991 Population Census. The variations in population growth in the 1990s will have no impact on the employment situation in that decade as the additional people will be too young to join the labour force. But the likely prospect of entering the twenty-first century with continuing high rates of growth in labour supply reinforces the National Manpower Commission's stress on population policy as the highest priority for the 1990s.

(b) Changes due to greater availability of school and training places:

The simulation brings out a significant change to be expected in the 1990s in the pattern of people leaving school. Education statistics in the late 1980s show a surge of primary school enrollments. Applying standard drop-out rates to these enrollments give results which point to a great rise in people with completed primary schooling (usually identified with "literacy" in Pakistan). This increase will only have a small effect on the aggregate labour supply, as primary schooling is almost complete by the age of 10 and the drop-out rate between primary and secondary schooling is high. But the schooling pattern of the labour supply may change dramatically in the 1990s without further government initiatives at the primary schooling level. The National Manpower Commission's strong support for universal primary education is probably being expressed in people's own planning for their children, though whether this increased demand is being adequately publicly resourced to improve, or even maintain, the quality of primary schools is an important policy issue.

(c) Changes due to labour force participation rates:

The simulation converts the "labour pools" of people aged 10 or over with various levels of schooling into a final labour supply through the operation of special Labour Force Participation Rates. These rates are set at levels for women and girls of 10 or over of all schooling levels, excluding students, to give results for the late 1980s in line with Labour Force Survey statistics at about 10 per cent economically active, with higher rates for "illiterate" women and "higher educated" women to reflect "need to work" and "want to work" pressures respectively. For all men and boys aged 10 or over, under 65, and not in education, the rates used, if adjusted for student numbers, would be about 90 per cent.

The precise rates were calculated to calibrate the simulation to generate an open unemployment rate of between 3 and 3.5 per cent in 1987. There is a stronger case for upward revision of these calibration rates than downward. The reasons for upward revision would include the data bias towards underestimation of women's economic activity (examined at length in the next Chapter) as well as the possibilty of more women offering themselves for employment, if encouraged by labour market buoyancy or policy initiatives. There is some case for downwards revision if people were discouraged from offering their labour by labour market depression or restrictive policy, but economic necessity sets a firm floor to such "discouragement" for most people in Pakistan.

The National Manpower Commission also sees more reasons for Labour Force Participation Rates to rise rather than fall in the 1990s, and makes many concrete recommendations which will encourage greater participation by women; recommendations totally consistent with its concern for reducing population growth rates.

(d) Changes due to international return migration:

The simulation implicitly assumes zero net labour force emigration or immigration. The Seventh Five Year Plan and the National Manpower Commission report assume 0.4 million net returnees in 1993. But a pessimistic assumption that the net numbers of people involved are not significant is justifiable. In macro-economic terms, the remittances associated with emigration will continue to be very significant.The National Manpower Commission is rightly very concerned about the productive use of these remittances, especially by returning migrants themselves in generating self-employment and small-scale wage employment.

2.3 The Changing Demands for People to Enter Employment

(a) Aggregate GDP growth induced employment:

An annual aggregate investment rate of 18.7 percent distributed on the sectoral pattern of the 1980s yields a simulated GDP real growth rate of just over 6 per cent per annum throughout the 1990s, a rate warranted by the actual performance in the late 1980s. This growth is led by the manufacturing and commerce sectors, with services growing in value-added terms slightly ahead of the aggregate GDP rate. Thus there is an implicit assumption that government expenditure will grow at, but only at, the rate of GDP growth in the 1990s.

The Seventh Five Year Plan envisages growth of GDP at between 6 and 7 per cent and the National Manpower Commission emphasises that the employment situation requires expansionary macro-economic policies aimed at achieving GDP growth rates of 7 per cent per annum or more. And even such a growth rate would still require specific policies on maintaining or increasing employment elasticities with respect to GDP growth if the growing labour supply is to be productively absorbed. In response to the prospect of increasing unemployment shown in Table 2.2, the Seventh Plan adopts a similar approach as shown in Table

2.3. Kemal (1990) analyses the Seventh Plan proposals using regression techniques and finds the Plan conclusions tending significantly to the optimistic side.

TABLE 2.2

Quantitative Projections of Employment in the Seventh Plan

(in millions)

	Estimated July 1988	Estimated July 1993
Population	105.4	122.8
Domestic Labour Force	31.0	36.1
Net Returnees	—	0.4
Total Labour Force	31.0	36.5
Unemployment	1.1	2.4
Employment	29.9	34.1
Unemployment (% of Labour Force)	3.5	6.6

Note: Estimates are based on crude activity rate of 29.4 per cent as given in the LFS of 1986-87.

TABLE 2.3

Employment Generation in the Seventh Plan

(million additional jobs)

(1)	(2)	(3)
1.	Employment increase associated with 6.5 per cent growth in GDP	4.2
2.	Programme for the rehabilitation of return migrants	0.35
3.	Additional employment generation 10-Point Employment Strategy:	—
	— Additional employment due to industrial promotion policies and emphasis on use of local engineering goods.	0.15
	— Small-Scale industry	0.55
	— Self-Employment promotion scheme	0.15
	— Skill-generation programmes	0.2
	— Rural employment policies	0.2
	— Others including the employment effect of promoting construction and consultancy service.	0.3
Total		6.1

Source: *Seventh Five Year Plan 1988-93*, Planning Commission, Government of Pakistan, undated.

(b) Sectoral value-added elasticities of employment and the prospects for different sectors:

The simulation divides total investment between nine sectors in the pattern of the 1980s (11.0 per cent agriculture, 1.9 per cent mining, 17.6 per cent manufacturing, 4.1 per cent construction, 11.9 per cent electricity, 11.2 per cent transport, 0.8 per cent commerce, 13.5 per cent finance, and 27.9 per cent services). These sectors have very different labour absorptive characteristics both in terms of employment elasticity with respect to value-added and labour productivity. The Seventh Five Year Plan does propose some adjustment towards higher employment elasticity sectors and areas within sectors. But the National Manpower Commission is equally concerned to raise overall labour productivity and not encourage low-productivity "employment-creation" in low productivity sectors. On balance, the pattern of sectoral distribution is not an active policy matter and therefore the simulation assumptions are justified.

(c) Technology choice within sectors:

Within sectors, the simulation assumes for all sectors a steady movement of about two percent per annum towards greater use of fixed capital per unit of output and less of labour per unit of output. The National Manpower Commission points to the possibility that agriculture and manufacturing have been over-encouraged to mechanise in the past by input pricing (including exchange rate) and credit policies. But the Commission recognises that depressing labour productivity in order to create jobs is not desirable and that large-scale units will remain mechanised and may have to further mechanise if they are to be internationally competitive.

The Commission therefore puts emphasis on new, small-scale establishments being set up which by their very technical and economic nature will use less fixed capital per workplace. Such a shift at the margin of establishment creation would affect the assumptions in the simulation. Many of the recommendations in the National Manpower Commission report and in Chapter 6 are aimed in this direction and thus try to increase productive labour demand above that reported in the simulation.

(d) International labour emigration:

As mentioned above, the simulation assumes no trend in international movement of Pakistani labour. The Seventh Plan envisages slight net return migration. The National Manpower Commission does see possibilities of increasing the quantity and raising the quality of labour emigration in the 1990s. The Commission argues that Pakistan lost out disproportionately from reduction in migrant labour demands from the Gulf region in the 1980s. This was due to the low skill profile (including English language) of Pakistani potential migrants compared to other countries' candidates and the lack of assertive Pakistani private and public sector presence in the labour recruiting countries.

The prospect of post-war reconstruction in Afghanistan, Iran and Iraq suggests possible renewed growth in the international labour market and the Commission makes policy recommendations to increase Pakistan's market share if the market does grow. These are to be supported—though with some caution given the fierce, experienced international competition. The simulation is implicitly pessimistic, and responsible, about this prospect and concentrates on domestic labour demand.

2.4 The Computer Simulation Labour Market Balances

The simulation results can be seen in terms of reported labour imbalances by levels of schooling and occupations. These imbalances can be negative, indicating a shortage of people readily available for economic activity with appropriate schooling for the pattern of occupations, or positive indicating a surplus of such people and a potential for underemployment as well as open unemployment.

In aggregate, the simulation reports a growing potential for open unemployment between 1987 and 2000 (see Table 2.4). The calibrated rate of 3.4 per cent in 1987 drifts out to a simulated rate of 7.4 per cent in the year 2000. There are periods of some respite between 1988 and 1990, 1996 to 1997, and 1999 to 2000, but unemployment pressures are tending to rise. This is an optimistic result compared with the results in World Bank 1989 and Kemal 1990 and yet still gives no reason for policy complacency.

TABLE 2.4

Simulation Model Results 1987-2000:
Labour Balance for Educational Level: All levels

Year	Nation		Balance	Per cent
	Supply	Demand		
1987	30003674	28990000	1013674	3.4
1988	30805711	29698768	1106942	3.6
1989	31558341	30415592	1142748	3.6
1990	32345109	31141198	1203911	3.7
1991	33234752	31877520	1357232	4.1
1992	34272798	32626370	1646428	4.8
1993	35309989	33389560	1920429	5.4
1994	36344784	34168388	2176395	6.0
1995	37356912	34964544	2392367	6.4
1996	38343398	35779263	2564135	6.7
1997	39220073	36613673	2606400	6.6
1998	40435207	37468810	2966397	7.3
1999	41536609	38345454	3191155	7.7
2000	42391268	39244250	3147018	7.4

Source: Cameron scenario of model described in Gulbrandsen 1990.

These pressures are felt unevenly between schooling levels. There is a shortage of people readily available for work among those who fail to complete primary school between 1987 and 1992, though the increasing educational demands built into the simulation turns this shortage into a growing surplus in the latter half of the 1990s (see Table 2.5).

The situation for those who complete primary schooling but drop out before the end of secondary school is very different. This group face heavy unemployment pressures throughout the whole period, though the tendency for the rate of unemployment to increase halts in the second half of the 1990s. It would appear that the current surge in taking up primary school places will have no parallel surge in the demand for the labour of people with only primary schooling (see Table 2.6).

For those who complete secondary schooling but not higher/tertiary education, the simulation shows substantial unemployment pressure in 1987 to 1989, but increasing shortages in the 1990s as the economy grows and becomes more technologically sophisticated. These shortages are becoming chronic by the year 2000 (see Table 2.7).

For higher/tertiary educated people, the pattern is also mixed. A trend towards increasing shortages up to 1992 is reversed in the second half of the 1990s as the current surge in primary educated people trickles through into higher education graduates (see Table 2.8).

The pattern of occupational imbalances reveals more about the reasons for these different experiences. The current excess demand for people not completing primary school is primarily as rural workers and secondarily as industrial workers. As technology becomes more sophisticated and job-entry educational requirements shift, the demand for labour in all occupations, including rural and industrial workers leaps over those with only completed primary schooling education and

TABLE 2.5

Simulation Model Results 1987-2000:
Labour Balance for Educational Level: Pre-Primary

Year	Nation		Balance	Per cent
	Supply	Demand		
1987	17617615	18944170	–236555	–7.5
1988	18339358	19306583	–967225	–5.3
1989	18929868	19675952	–746084	–3.9
1990	19483842	20051936	–568094	–2.9
1991	20068204	20435554	–367350	–1.8
1992	20749427	20827840	–78413	–0.4
1993	21380338	21229839	150499	0.7
1994	21976410	21642273	334137	1.5
1995	22548924	22066121	482803	2.5
1996	23109211	22502079	607132	2.6
1997	23583929	22950787	633142	2.7
1998	24404233	23412833	991401	4.1
1999	25124301	2388648	1235653	4.9
2000	25604718	24378583	1226135	4.8

Source: Cameron scenario of model described in Gulbrandsen, 1990.

TABLE 2.6

Simulation Model Results 1987-2000:
Labour Balance for Educational Level: Primary

Year	Nation		Balance	Per cent
	Supply	Demand		
1987	6140090	4565755	1574335	25.6
1988	6298500	4724119	1574382	25.0
1989	6525606	4885914	1639692	25.1
1990	6808515	5051219	1757296	25.8
1991	7147189	5220151	1927038	27.0
1992	7519058	5392853	2126206	28.3
1993	7917299	5569525	2347774	29.7
1994	8323789	5750334	2573455	30.9
1995	8696554	5935545	2761008	31.7
1996	9029189	6125376	2903813	32.2
1997	9313131	6320044	2993087	32.1
1998	9576925	5619767	3057157	31.9
1999	9821609	6624731	3096878	31.5
2000	10052564	6935109	3117456	31.0

Source: Cameron scenario of model described in Gulbrandsen 1990.

TABLE 2.7

Simulation Model Results 1987-2000:
Labour Balance for Educational Level: Secondary

Year	Nation		Balance	Per cent
	Supply	Demand		
1987	4827627	4066636	760991	15.8
1988	4703706	4164729	538977	11.5
1989	4588495	4259621	328874	7.2
1990	4483283	4352003	131280	2.9
1991	4385413	4442380	–56967	–1.3
1992	4296127	4531108	–234981	–5.5
1993	4213590	4618467	–404876	–9.6
1994	4140601	4704608	–564007	–13.6
1995	4075402	4789695	–714292	–17.5
1996	4012480	4873791	–861312	–21.5
1997	3948509	4956920	–1008410	–25.5
1998	3880257	5039064	–1158807	–29.9
1999	3812349	5120157	–1307808	–34.3
2000	3742933	5200092	–1457159	–38.9

Source: Cameron scenario of model described in Gulbrandsen, 1990.

TABLE 2.8

Simulation Model Results 1987-2000:
Labour Balance for Educational Level: Higher

Year	Nation		Balance	Per cent
	Supply	Demand		
1987	1418343	1413440	4903	0.3
1988	1464146	1503337	–39191	–2.7
1989	1514371	1594105	–79734	–5.3
1990	1569469	1686040	–116571	–7.4
1991	1633945	1779434	–145489	–8.9
1992	1708185	1874568	–166383	–9.7
1993	1798761	1971729	–172968	–9.6
1994	1903984	2071173	–167189	–8.8
1995	2036031	2173184	–137152	–6.7
1996	2192518	2278017	–85499	–3.9
1997	2374504	2385922	–11418	–0.5
1998	2573791	2497145	–76646	3.0
1999	2778350	2611919	166431	6.0
2000	2991053	2730467	260586	8.7

Source. Cameron scenario of model described in Gulbrandsen 1990

picks up those people with completed secondary schooling. But, in the simulation, this increasing sophistication is not sufficient to create adequate demand for the increasing numbers of people completing higher education.

In conclusion, the simulation model shows a version of Pakistan's future which can be read alongside the more pessimistic World Bank 1989 and Kemal 1990 results. The demand-side reveals a shift from a technology capable of employing unschooled people in large numbers towards one hungry for people with about ten years of schooling. On the supply side, the simulation finds an autonomous process of growth in people offering five years of schooling. The shift process is complicated with movements from shortages to surpluses for each education level grouping of people, apart from the primary educated people who are always in surplus. If policy were to be guided by responses to immediate data signals, then the simulation suggests the following chronology:

1987-1990: concerns about unemployment among primary and secondary educated people, some tightness in rural labour markets;

1991-1993: concerns about unemployment among primary educated and growth in overall unemployment, shortages emerging in professional, administrative, and technician occupations with educational policy implications for expanding secondary and higher education;

1994-1997: continuing concerns about unemployed primary educated people and continuing rise in overall unemployment, heavy demands for secondary educated people in professional, administrative and technician occupations but excess demand for higher educated abating;

1998-2000: unemployment emerging among those who have not completed primary education (poverty implications) and the higher educated (aspiration frustration implications). In a separate simulation ending in the year 2003, Herman and Irfan attempted to assess the emerging situation in the labour market (Herman and Irfan 1990). Using the existing labour force data, they estimate unemployment rates rising from five per cent in 1989 to 11 per cent in 1998 (in about the middle of the World Bank 1989 range). An interesting implication of the projection exercise is that they estimate around 40 per cent of those with education of matriculation and above who will enter into the labour force will not get a job, i.e. 40 per cent of the incremental labour force of this group will be unemployed. Clearly, such conclusions are very sensitive to the mapping between education and occupations which is not merely a matter of optimal technical qualifications (an issue discussed in Kemal 1990).

This projection exercise also reports results including Seventh Plan policy proposals such as increased recruitment of teachers. The exercise concludes that even in the extreme case of achieving the objective of universal primary education resulting in massive recruitment of teachers, this will exhaust itself as a source of new employment in a decade or so.

This underscores the importance of understanding that crash programme policy responses may be only short term palliatives on the labour demand side which can only be regarded as providing a breathing space. Also, arguably, this projection shows an upper boundary to the possible range of unemployment rates for the educated.

On the basis of these simulations, policy would be mistaken to over-react to rural labour shortages through encouraging mechanisation in the late 1980s, mistaken to expand higher education on a crash-programme basis in the mid-1990s, and mistaken to stress expansion of primary education at the expense of secondary education throughout the period.

But the simulations do not allow for second round feedbacks into the change process as people learn and market forces operate on the first round imbalances. The historical evidence in Chapter 1 shows examples of such feedbacks in Pakistan suggesting a significant amount of flexible adjustability to changing experiences.

2.5 Second Round Feedbacks into the Labour Market

(a) Rural-rural and rural-urban migration (rural and urban infrastructure development):

A primary response to unemployment or low-paid/unpaid economic activity is to move to a more promising location. More promising often means a more active labour market with the possibility of higher earnings, not necessarily a labour market with clear labour shortages and unfilled vacancies. A critical mass of urban population has now probably been reached in Pakistan so that most rural dwellers have a first contact in urban areas. Rural primary-educated unemployment and under-employment can relatively easily turn itself into urban under-employment or unemployment.

The public sector costs of non-productive urbanisation are high in terms of all kinds of infrastructure provision. The National Manpower Commission recognises this fact, and recommends rural infrastructure provision and positive initiatives in rural small-scale industry development in order to make productive rural employment increasingly available. But there must be doubts about the ability of such policies to stem the flow of primary educated young men to the cities as speculative job seekers and an urban policy with respect to such people will also be needed.

(b) Education/skills/occupational responses:

The simulation maps directly and mechanically from a distribution of education levels to occupations. But, in practice, this mapping is neither as direct or as mechanical and there may be strong second round feedback effects. Flexibility lies predominantly in the direction of people eventually being willing to move into occupations for which they appear to be educationally over-qualified.

Thus, unemployment pressure can be displaced onto the lower formally educated. But such a pressure is not automatic insofar as a level of education is psychologically and socially associated with occupations having a certain status. But it is likely that such prestige considerations delay rather than totally block the process of displacement over a period as long as a decade. But, nevertheless, adjustment can be both painful, resented, and politically sensitive.

But such supply-side adjustment is only half the story. If the pressure will be primarily on rural primary educated young men, how will agricultural employers feel about replacing relatively compliant non-schooled workers with resentful, frustrated primary school educated workers with little, if any, productivity gain? The answer is probably "without enthusiasm"!

On a similar basis, it may be that secondary educated people will not displace lower educated people, both because they feel the work offered is beneath them and employers' reluctance to hire potentially more troublesome workers. But the continuing large labour productivity gains envisaged in the manufacturing, electricity, transport, commerce, and finance sectors would arguably be difficult to achieve without some upgrading in educational requirements and thus employers in those sectors will have stronger incentives to employ more highly educated people than at the present and the resources to reward them better than current employees, if necessary.

This may in turn encourage more primary school completers to continue to completion of secondary schooling. Drop-out rates between primary and secondary school levels will then be lower in the 1990s than in the 1980s. This will mean more people in full-time education than envisaged in the simulation and a reduction in the unemployment pressure in the 1990s, especially on the primary educated. This beneficial feedback will need increased resources in secondary schooling and assumes that the total opportunity costs of continuing in school are not unacceptably high for many households.

Thus the labour market odds may still be weighted heavily against those with only primary schooling, especially younger men. However, there is a crucial step between completed secondary schooling and occupation (and between completed non-vocational higher education and occupation), which the simulation omits and may offer "late-start" opportunities to even out unemployment pressures.

The acquisition of occupational skills is not part of secondary schooling. Changing attitudes and forms of specific occupational training provide an opportunity for those with lower schooling levels to enter, and those with higher schooling to miss out on, employment in occupations compared to the simulation results.

The simulation's mapping of a distribution of educational levels into each occupation on the basis of 1980s data may be sensitive to policy development in skill training and perceptions of that training, especially the rigidity of age and educational qualification requirements for entry. The National Manpower Commission faces this issue by recommending that rigidities in skill training provision be reduced and a much more interactive, integrated approach be adopted bringing public sector training, private sector training, and private and public sector employers together. Such flexibility should serve to even out imbalances in the labour market and, perhaps, allow greater numbers of primary educated people to come into occupations showing shortages in the mid and late 1990s, than envisaged in the simulation.

(c) Changing real rates of return to occupations and casualisation:

The simulation does not allow for the standard market forces feedback through changing real rates of return in response to imbalances. Pakistan has had a number of studies and surveys focusing upon the wages and living conditions of workers, particularly those working in the large scale manufacturing sector, which have revealed significant flexibility.

A. R. Khan assessed the movement of industrial workers' real wage movement during 1954-67 (Khan 1987). He viewed that the real wages of industrial workers declined during the period under study at a time when labour supply was rising relatively fast compared to demand at a time when large-scale industry was being emphasised.

Adopting a wider definition of wages by including non-cash benefits, Guisinger and Irfan examined the movement of real wages of industrial workers and concluded that real wages improved during 1954-70 (Guisinger and Irfan 1974). Capital intensity, labour productivity and unionism were found to be the main influencing factors. Irfan also examined the impact of participation of an industry in international trade, and its domestic market concentration on workers' wages and found that the level of protection enjoyed by an industry positively influences its wage level, while dependence on export demand tends to depress wage levels (Irfan 1979).

Very few research efforts aimed at examination of employment or wages in the single largest sector of the economy, agriculture, have been made, but generally they do show evidence of real wage flexibility. Jerry Eckert conducted a survey during 1970-71 in Punjab wherein he collected operation specific data in the crop sector of farming (Eckert 1972). Hira Shima during the early seventies conducted a small survey in Punjab (Shima 1980). His focus was both on farm and non-farm households and the quantum of employment generated by the farm sector for the non-farm population. More recently Mehboob Elahi and Jameel Khan conducted a survey of 450 households (285 farm and 165 non-farm). The study highlighted the importance of cropping pattern and cropping intensity for labour demand (Elahi and Khan 1986). In addition, the authors viewed that the demand for hired labour input in crop related activities is rather inelastic with respect to changes in wage rates, suggesting supply side determination of wage rates.

Employment implications of varying tenurial system and land distributions have also been studied showing more people being pushed into a relatively open, competitive labour market. S. M. Naseem and Akmal Hussain dealt with these issues (Naseem 1981 and Hussain 1988). Hussain highlighted the growing landlessness occasioned by the resumption of land by owners. A significant decline in the tenancy and drastic reduction in the number of permanent farm work during 1971-80 also emerges as a major conclusion of a study on landlessness in Pakistan conducted by Irfan (Irfan 1985). Studies on structure of wages encompassing all the sectors of the economy are even rarer. Rahman in 1969-70 tried to compare the wage structure in government and non-government formal organizations (Rahman 1970). Guisinger, Hicks and Pilvin examined the long term income trends and wages in different sectors and concluded that in general real wages had risen during the 1960s (Guisinger, Hicks and Pilvin 1977). Irfan and Meekal Ahmed extended this line of enquiry and assessed the impact of emigration on wage levels in the domestic labour market (Irfan and Ahmed 1985). One of the major conclusions was that Gulf region migration led to tightening of the labour market, resulting in rises in real wages which may have been responsible for rising capital intensity in the economy, including agriculture.

Overall, the impression from work on wage rates in Pakistan does suggest flexibility but no clear tendency to complete market-clearing in terms of second round physical supply or demand side feedbacks with dramatic changes in people offering or withdrawing work and/or changes in numbers of jobs offered. It seems likely that choices are restricted both for people entering or leaving occupations, and employers choosing techniques of production. The distribution of incomes may change, but the amount of employment may be relatively inflexible.

Thus the impact of the simulation results of growing pressures towards unemployment in the 1990s could be a downward pressure on real wage rates across the whole economy but resulting in neither people withdrawing from economic activity nor significant shifts towards more labour-intensive techniques or more labour-intensive sectors. Existing employers would collect windfall gains in their existing lines of activity and new entrants would enter those lines in response to that increased profitability choosing the same profitable technique of production (assuming there is an actual choice in technique available). Pockets of resistance to the general downward pressure on wage rates will be met by increasingly powerful employers through various forms of contracting out and casualisation.

Some occupations with shortages of technically necessary, appropriately educated applicants may attract premium earnings rates at various times in the 1990s. But ceilings will be set on those premiums by the temporary nature of the shortages and the general willingness of employers in Pakistan, given the low income of the average domestic consumer, to accept lower quality of work and output if unit costs can be reduced.

Market forces, working through the labour pricing mechanism, are likely only weakly to counter the overall and specific labour market imbalances predicted by the simulation. The National Manpower Commission does envisage a role for competitive market forces in ensuring that employed labour is used productively and efficiently, though "responsible" trades unionism has a role to play in improving health and safety and moderating mere distributional shifts of "rents" to monopoly employers in the private or public sectors.

The Commission appears much less confident that market forces will induce sufficient employment through increasing labour-intensity within sectors or sufficient shifts towards more labour-intensive sectors. Getting the prices right in the labour market is judged insufficient to ensure employment for all who are ready to be economically active in Pakistan in the 1990s.

2.6 Implications of the Scenario Results for Open Educated Unemployment and Poverty in Practice

(a) Open educated unemployment:

The simulation results assume close and immediate matching of people graduating at a specific educational level and the filling of a vacancy in an occupation requiring that educational level. In practice, this matching is the result of a search process which depends upon objective information and subjective attitudes. As the aggregate labour market tightens then everyone seeking fresh economic activity feels some of the strain as objective information on vacancies becomes harder to find and subjective attitudes become more negative. For those who can afford not to work for a period as they possess consumption rights in a relatively affluent household, open unemployment may result, even though the simulation accurately predicts job possibilities for people with those qualifications.

Evidence on such open unemployment is found in a recently conducted survey of the "Quantification of Unemployment among Educated Youth in Pakistan" in Karachi. A detailed socio-economic survey of a random sample of 6285 households in Karachi undertaken by the Applied Economics Research Centre attempted to assess the unemployment situation in the city in 1987 (Applied Economics Research Centre, 1989). The overall unemployment rate in Karachi was found to be around 10 per cent. People without schooling claimed a lower rate of measured employment (7.8 per cent) in comparison to people with schooling (10.3 per cent) but undoubtedly many of those without schooling in employment were still in absolute poverty. Around 12 per cent of secondary school matriculates and 8 percent of higher educated degree holders and post graduate persons were found to be without employment.

A survey conducted by Gallup (Pakistan) Ltd. for the National Manpower Commission in 1989 also suggested high rates of unemployment among the highly educated. Information on employment status of graduates was gathered through a mailed questionnaire with a response rate of around 42 per cent. A finding of the survey was that 36.4 per cent of responding graduates and higher educated were unemployed. In addition, 25 per cent of the graduates who were identified as employed declared themselves as looking for a better job. This suggests that more than half of the respondents were dissatisfied either through being unemployed or unhappy with their present employment.

Of those who were employed, around half waited for more than a year before finding suitable work. The highest employment rate was found among BScs and Bachelors of Commerce. Roughly half of the medical doctors were also found unemployed while one-third of engineers were without a job.

Even if one were to adjust the reported unemployment rate in the survey for the non-response, the resulting estimates would be still far from the situation predicted in the simulation for 1989 with a higher education shortage of 5.3 per cent.

But this is not a new phenomenon, studies aimed at the quantification of unemployment among educated youth were also conducted during 1968-72. Abdul Aziz Anwar's "Problems of Unemployment among Educated Manpower" was a tracer study of the graduates of Punjab University, Lahore, West Pakistan University of Engineering and Technology, Lahore, and West Pakistan Agricultural University, Faisalabad (Anwar 1973). In his postal enquiry 900 out of 1900 respondents reported themselves to be unemployed. Moreover, the unemployment rate among non-professionals was found to be two and half times higher than professionals. Similarly, unemployment among educated women was reported to be 50 per cent higher than their less educated contemporaries. One of the major limitations of this study was a very low response rate which seriously casts doubt about the validity of the findings. van Lent assessed the unemployment of Lahore Polytechnic graduates of the two years of 1967-69 (van Lent 1971). The average unemployment rate after 12 months on the labour market, was estimated to be 40 percent. Rado, who was also critical of this study, re-estimated this rate to be around 30 per cent. Interestingly half of the respondents expressed their dissatisfaction with their practical training. Moreover, those "successful" in having a job were found to be earning on average Rs. 243 which at that time was not substantially higher than the wage rate of unskilled workers.

There were other "surveys of technical manpower" sponsored by the National Manpower Council. A major limitation of most of these surveys was their coverage problem. A small proportion of those who had been sent questionnaires through the post actually responded. This highlights the difficulties involved in postal enquiries and the problems of tracer surveys and a possible bias towards over-estimating unemployment. These surveys presented an estimation of unemployment among technically trained persons ranging from 16.3 per cent to 39 per cent.

Thus recording higher rates of open unemployment among the educated than seem warranted by general labour market conditions is not a recent phenomenon in Pakistan. The problem is how to distinguish (in order of policy accessibility):

(i) Lack of objective information on all possible vacancies;

(ii) Lack of specific skills required to turn an educational qualification into an occupational qualification;

(iii) Willingness and resources to undertake a prolonged search for the best terms and conditions available;

(iv) Unrealistic, and very reluctantly adapting, expectations of salary, other benefits, career prospects, working conditions and/or location of work.

The National Manpower Commission recommends that Employment Exchanges be strengthened as information centres and that all training involve potential employers to ensure employability of graduates. With respect to prolonged searches and unrealistic expectations, it is important that policy statements and token programmes do not prolong the process of search or encourage unrealistic hopes. In such circumstances, short-run crash programmes can do serious longer-run damage.

Underemployment in terms of time and rates of earnings has received much less attention than open unemployment. Estimates have been made on the basis of number of hours worked as provided by Labour Force Surveys. But there are questions about the meaning, policy relevance and validity of these time-based estimates in understanding labour availability and poverty. It is understanding underemployment better which will probably give greater insights into poverty in Pakistan.

(b) Poverty:

There have been a number of studies aimed primarily at the quantification of numbers of people in poverty in Pakistan. These studies have followed the conventional approach of trying to estimate the number of people defined to have incomes or consumption levels below an arbitrary poverty line. Household Income and Expenditure Surveys indicate that the proportion of the population living below a poverty line defined by an income inconsistent with consuming 2550 calories per person per day went down during the 1970s and 1980s. Both the inflow of remittances and the growth of the economy as well as closely associated rising real wages could be identified as the major factors responsible for this change.

With the interlinked curtailment in the inflow of remittances, stagnation or decline in real wage rates and increasing labour market imbalance, it cannot be expected that this declining trend in the incidence of poverty will continue in the 1990s. The supply pressures in the labour market in 1990s are likely to lead to falling real wage rates as the demand side pressures led to rising real wage rates in the 1980s. It seems fair to assume that many of those on the margins of poverty are centrally engaged in the market economy and their fortunes will fluctuate with the market value of unskilled labour, whether or not they are formally unemployed.

In order to trace quantitatively the effects of increasing labour market imbalances on the poverty situation, there is a need to measure the importance of wage income and employment in poverty alleviation. It must be pointed out that a precise estimate of the income due to labour as a factor cannot be made because Household Income and Expenditure Surveys provide data on income from different sources in a form from which it is difficult to allocate a share to labour in the income reported under self employment or business. A perusal of these surveys, however, does indicate that wage income as a proportion of total income is higher for the lower income groups and its importance declines as one moves up the income scale.

There is a real risk of a rise in the incidence of employed poverty both in urban as well as in rural areas in the 1990s. Thus the emerging situation in practice could involve more poverty for employed people as well as more frustration and poverty for the unemployed, who will not always be consuming at poverty levels if they live in supportive households.

Take-up of facilities provided by the state in the fields of health and education may also be a positive function of household income levels. If people are constrained in meeting nutrition needs, it is possible that their use of schools or the health system will not increase since both involve an element of cost to the household, thus further lowering the members' quality of life.

2.7 Conclusions

Barring dramatic exogenous positive changes at the global level, the simulation model, analysis of feedbacks, and discussion of unemployment and poverty in practice indicate a prognosis for the Pakistan labour market in the 1990s which hardly augurs well for Pakistan society.

The unabated population growth of the past decade with the implication that the labour force will grow at more than three per cent per annum throughout the 1990s means that Pakistan enters into the 1990s with labour market conditions and processes which appear more unpromising and threatening than the previous crisis period of the early 1970s and with as little state planning room for manoeuvre.

As it is unlikely that another "Gulf region boom" will rescue the situation in the 1990s as it did in the 1970s, there is a clear need for new initiatives in well-informed, cost-effective, state planning working with people's planning utilising Pakistan's resources to generate more, more productive employment.

CHAPTER 3

Improving the Labour Market Information System

3.1 The Data Needs of an Enabling Government

An enabling government will be less involved in direct employment creation and human resource development than a government stressing state planning but more involved than a government relying on market forces and people's planning governed solely by those forces.

The enabling approach is very demanding in terms of an information system. The operation of the state itself will not generate required information as it might in a heavily state planned approach, where ministries and departments had direct responsibilities for employment and training. But neither can the government rely on a few macro-indicators to modify policy as it might with a fully market-led approach. An enabling government acts, but acts at a distance. State planners allocate resource inputs to line ministries and departments whose outputs in turn become the inputs into people's plans which produce new outputs that the state planners need to monitor and evaluate to gauge policy effectiveness and feedback into revised resource allocations to line ministries and departments.

The monitoring and evaluation activities must include systematic, representative, independent surveys as well as more ad hoc line ministry and department and community assessments. The National Manpower Commission has tended to stress information gathered by line ministries and departments in the course of their day-to-day operations. The IMF has insisted on monitoring only a few aggregate macro-economic performance indicators. The current authors' concern is with monitoring and evaluating people's actual activities and experience at an appropriate level of detail for policy purposes through regular surveys.

At the outset, it must be said that the present situation in Pakistan appears very weak in this area. There are gaps, conceptualisation inadequacies, non-representativeness, and delays in information availability across all sectors. It might be said that Pakistan's labour market information system is constructed as if the state planners directly control all significant areas of economic activity in a reality where most activity is conducted on market terms (though not necessarily open competitive markets) and is ignored by or intentionally bypasses the state.

We feel the conclusions in the first two chapters are robust enough to stand likely data inaccuracies, apart from employment in large scale manufacturing and women's labour force participation rates, but have no confidence in the current labour market information system for detailed policy development by an enabling government.

3.2 The Present Labour Market Information System

A number of institutions and organisations are engaged in the collection and dissemination of employment and labour force data. A cursory glance at the various surveys and reports would tend to make one believe that most of the required information for policy formulation is available. However, this is far from true. The real problem emerges when one tries to interpret the data or operationalise policy actions in terms of the actual collected information when it becomes available.

The available data sources can be classified both according to periodicity and frequency of publication and by using the classifications of the intended coverage of the exercises. Below, we briefly describe the available data sources.

(a) Population Censuses:

Decennial Population Censuses constitute a major source of information on population and its distribution as well as broad sectoral occupational classifications. Four Population Censuses have been conducted in Pakistan. An inter-temporal comparison of the data provided by Population Censuses cannot be adequately made between Censuses themselves or between Censuses and other surveys because of the changes both in conceptualisation as well as enumeration methodology. For instance, the labour force participation rate recorded by 1981 Population Census is based on usual employment status while the Housing, Economic and Demographic Survey of 1973 adopted current (i.e. a reference week) labour force approach. It may also be noted that unlike the 1961 Population Census, where total enumeration was used to obtain data on employment, the subsequent Censuses used a sample survey simultaneously to arrive at the employment and unemployment estimates.

(b) Agricultural Censuses:

Agricultural Censuses are also conducted approximately every ten years which provide information on land distribution and cropping patterns as well as employment of the work force in agriculture and livestock activities on a national basis. Because of the fact that an Agricultural Census has particular objectives, the employment data are generally collected through usage of concepts which are substantially at variance with the Population Censuses or Labour Force Surveys. Thus rural or agricultural employment estimated on the basis of Agricultural Censuses differ widely with that one would obtain from Population Censuses or their associated 10 per cent post-censal sample surveys. It must be said that the labour force participation rates recorded in Agricultural Censuses are much higher and much more plausible than those recorded in Population Censuses.

(c) Labour Force Surveys (LFS):

Labour Force Surveys constitute the most commonly used major source of information on employment, its sectoral and regional distribution, and unemployment. The Labour Force Survey is based on a representative sample and technically can provide ratio estimates on different characteristics of the population. But there is a growing perception that the unemployment rate as well as the female labour force participation rate provided by these Surveys are seriously underestimated. It would be informative to note that specialised studies aimed at quantification of the unemployment among educated youth conducted during the early 70s as well as during 1989 provided substantially different data estimates of unemployment among educated youth than the Labour Force Surveys. Similarly, studies specifically focusing upon women's work pattern and participation in the household activities provide a widely divergent picture regarding participation rates than the impression from the Labour Force Surveys.

Most of these problems are generally attributed to inadequacy of the concepts used to define a person as economically active. In addition, it must be noted that the sample size of the Labour Force Surveys is often small and inadequate in rendering guidance for any investigation attempting to focus on minority subgroups.

(d) The Census of Manufacturing Industries (CMI):

The CMI constitutes the major source for information on large scale manufacturing industries (defined by a ten employee or more registration requirement). In principle, the CMI provides information both on employment as well as on employment cost at the international three digit level of standard industrial classification. It does not provide data on the occupational breakdown by level of education of the employed. The CMI is an annual postal survey and generally reported to have suffered from non-response. Also publication is usually several years after data collection.

A Systems (Pvt) Ltd. and Fareedy's study (Systems Ltd 1990 and Fareedy 1990) highlights that there is unreporting and non-reporting of employment, notably contract employment, but also regular workers, by enterprises actually making returns. If such under-reporting amount to the one-third indicated in the Systems (Pvt.) Ltd. survey then many calculations of the size of the small-scale manufacturing industrial sector and the capital intensity of the large-scale manufacturing sector are thrown into question.

(e) Annual Establishment Enquiry (AEE):

The Provincial Labour Directorates are meant to conduct annual establishment enquiries of all employing enterprises. The information is collected through mailed questionnaires including requests for data on employment by occupation and by sector of the economy. Data on wages paid are also requested. In practice, these surveys are generally confined to the large-scale sector of the economy (establishments with more than 10 employees). In principle, one can use these surveys to infer changes in levels of employment and other aspects of the labour market such as wages. However, less than satisfactory coverage, and non-availability or delays in making data public poses problems. In addition, not all the Provinces regularly conduct these surveys.

(f) Other Data Sources:

Data collected as a part of monitoring the implementation of labour laws constitute another source of information on the labour market, though its coverage and accuracy is always likely to be compromised by the possible legal implications of data revelation. Nine returns are submitted to the Provincial Labour Directorates relating to the following set of labour laws and regulations: (i) Factories Act 1934, (ii) Shops and Establishment Ordinance 1959, (iii) West Pakistan Industrial and Commercial Employment Standing Order Ordinance 1968, (iv) Industrial Relations Ordinance 1969, (v) Workman's Compensation Act 1923, (vi) Maternity Benefits Ordinance, 1958, (vii) Payment of Wages Act in Factories in 1936, (viii) Annual Report on Contract Labour, (ix) Payment of Wages Act 1936.

Annual consolidated reports of the working of labour laws in Pakistan detail the data collected under these labour regulations, through mailed enquiry. The data pertains to level of employment, broken down by sex of the workers and size of the firm, wages, daily breaks, holidays and hours of work, frequency of inspections, number of industrial disputes and number of accidents and compensation paid. One can also obtain some information on contract labour and trade unions in these reports.

Furthermore, two returns under the Mines Act 1923 and Excise Duty on Minerals are also submitted to the Provincial Labour Directorate which provide data on number of persons employed, output of minerals, accidents according to classification of mines, employment and amount of compensation. A return from Karachi Port Trust on dock labour under the Dock Labourers' Act of 1934 and Dock Labourers' Notification regulations of 1948 provide data on ships inspected and the number of accidents.

Employment exchanges provide information on registered job seekers and vacancies. However, due to the fact that this data is client-initiated, the representativeness and quality of this data can hardly be regarded as adequate for policy formulation. The National Manpower Commission recommends strengthening Employment Exchanges with wider terms of reference as basic units in the Labour Market Information System. While this is desirable, it cannot substitute totally for more systematically representative surveys.

Other surveys are conducted occasionally which are not a regular or annual feature, but do provide some information on labour market. For instance, surveys conducted by Federal Bureau of Statistics on transport and distributive trades fall under this category. Data on the vital small-scale manufacturing sector has been collected only in 1976/7, 1983/4 and 1986/7 (due to be possibly published in 1990) by the Federal Bureau of Statistics leaving this sector's performance generally to be estimated by residual methods rather than direct observation.

3.3 Clarifying Conceptualisation

Much debate on employment and labour force patterns in Pakistan is forced to stop at the point of disputing the conceptualisation and accuracy of the major official data series. The perception that the concepts and measures used to estimate labour supply in the developing world are inadequate is hardly new. Precisely, at the time when these concepts and the current labour force approach was being advocated for application in the developing world, there were people who pointed out the inadequacy of these concepts. For example, Jaffe and Stewart in their book *Manpower Resources and Utilization* in 1951 were critical of the application of US labour force survey procedures to Puerto Rico and Japan (Jaffe and Stewart 1951). W. E. Moore in an article entitled *The Exportability of the Labour Force Concept* counselled for application of care in using a labour force approach in the developing world (Moore 1953). D. Turnhaume in a book *The Employment Problem in Less Developed Countries in* 1971 stated that time and money were being misallocated to elaborate comment and high powered analysis of incredibly inadequate source material (Turnhaume 1971). The limitations of these concepts for their applicability to the developing world have been succinctly summarised by Standing (Standing 1978).

The inadequacy of these concepts mostly stems from a lack of correspondence between the economic reality of the developing world and the international standard approaches to perception and conceptualisation. The major issues involved arise from the application of the notion of economic activity very often couched in terms like "job", "occupation", or "employed". In a milieu where consumption and production can hardly be differentiated household economic activities may dovetail with domestic work and blur the border line between so-called economic and non-economic activities.

Furthermore, a rigid labour force approach can hardly reflect adequately the fluid and dynamic situation of labour utilisation in an environment characterised by pervasive self employment and unpaid family help. In such a fluid situation where people switch from one category to another within reference periods, i.e. out of the labour force, into the labour force, employed and unemployed, the attempts to categorise uniquely may fail to depict the real situation and end up presenting results which are mostly a by-product of arbitrary applications of false dichotomies.

To be labelled "unemployed", the current approach implies that a person desires to have and be available for a full-time job without pre-conditions demonstrated through job search in a reference week. Meeting these restrictive requirements would define a person as unemployed in the economically `active' population. In the absence of regular channels for job search and social security systems, this conceptualisation of unemployment is very difficult to apply and has very little policy meaning taken in isolation.

It is internationally recognised that conventional definitions and associated approaches to measurement of economic activity which were developed for western economies returning to a male breadwinner approach to employment after World War II are especially inappropriate for women's activity everywhere. The conventional approach uses dichotomies of being wholly economically active or not, and, wholly in employment or fully unemployed. These dichotomies have no relevance to the realities of many women's lives in Pakistan.

A typical economic status interview will begin by asking the primary activity of each member of the household. The response "housewife" or "student" will be sufficient to label that person as economically inactive and of no further interest in the interview. The alternative, equally conceptually valid, question "does this person undertake any activity which contributes to the household's income in cash or kind inside or outside the home?" would almost certainly produce a very different pattern of responses and a higher Labour Force Participation Rate. Equally likely is the implicit assumption that an adult man must be economically active, even if "unemployed" or as an "unpaid family worker"

Current measurements of women's economic activity and Labour Force Participation Rates in Pakistan differ wildly depending on the source consulted (see Tables 3.1 and 3.2). This variation is an outcome of the method of measurement itself and probably bears no relationship to changes in the pattern of women's actual activities.

How far declared entry into the labour market is influenced by perceived job opportunities is difficult to quantify. The Labour Force Survey data however, may imply the presence of varying "discouraged worker effect" as well as measurement variations. For instance, the female labour force participation rate in the LFS rose from 6.4 per cent in 1974/75 to 11.8 per cent in 1978/79 with a subsequent decline to 8.7 per cent in 1984/85. The labour force participation rates of males falling in the age brackets of 10-14 and 15-19 recounts the same story. The rise in activity rates is experienced during the period when a massive exodus of labour to the Gulf region occurred and the labour market was considerably tightened and the fall when this phenomenon was weakening. But the basis of the data on women's labour force participation rates in the LFS is so weak that it is difficult to make any analysis with any confidence.

If the conventional dichotomy approach is to continue to be used in Pakistan then the case can easily be made that wide definitions should be adopted rather than the narrow definitions of economically active conventionally used. Not only will this be more just to women but will constitute a much more realistic basis for informed planning and policy-making for men and women.

In conceptualising underemployment, the few efforts that have been made have concentrated on time measurements. Underemployment in terms of income (poverty) has never been an integral part of the Labour Force Surveys. Poverty studies conducted in Pakistan, as in many countries, have been based on Household, Income and Expenditure Surveys and linking to forms of economic activity has consequent problems. Similarly, there have been few efforts to assess the extent employed persons are satisfied from their current job. The National Manpower Commission did attempt to estimate both time underemployment and job dissatisfaction (see Table 3.3).

The existing practices of collecting information on hours of work per reference period with the intention of determining under-employment particularly in rural areas and among the self-employed segment of the labour force can be misleading. In order to utilise such information for policy making, there has to be information on the seasonal labour demands of different crop rotations and the reward to the individual from the activity. If the objective is to alleviate poverty through making additional work available then data on labour peaks and marginal income and wage rates should supplement the data on labour time utilised.

TABLE 3.1

Estimates of Labour Force Participation Rates 1901-1987

Sources		Labour force as %age of Population	Crude Activity*		Refined Activity**	
			Male	Female	Male	Female
Population Census						
1901		34.8	57.0	8.5	—	—
1911		34.1	57.0	6.2	—	—
1921		33.3	56.1	5.4	—	—
1931		31.8	53.8	4.8	—	—
1951		30.60	55.1	2.1	79.4	3.1
Manpower Survey	1955	31.10	—	—	—	—
Population Census	1961	32.36	55.0	6.1	80.8	9.3
Labour Force Survey						
1963-64		32.60	—	—	—	—
1964-65		33.76	—	—	—	—
1966-67		33.45	57.62	6.71	86.7	10.3
1967-68		33.32	57.83	6.89	86.7	10.5
1968-69		29.49	52.40	4.36	79.0	6.6
1969-70		30.34	53.32	4.88	79.3	7.3
1970-71		30.41	53.13	5.43	80.0	8.1
1971-72		29.90	51.87	5.39	78.6	8.0
HEDS	1973	32.66	55.41	6.23	77.6	9.0
Labour Force Survey	1974-75	29.50	52.08	4.27	76.7	6.3
1978-79		31.02	57.25	7.01	77.3	11.8
Population Census	1981	27.60	50.6	2.14	72.5	3.2
Labour Force Survey						
1982-83		30.2	51.52	7.22	75.2	10.7
1984-85		29.60	51.68	5.80	77.1	8.7
1985-86		28.72	50.00	6.00	74.8	9.13
1986-87		29.40	49.50	7.9	73.5	11.9

* Crude activity rate is defined as number of persons in the labour force divided by the total population.

** Refined activity rate refers to number of persons in the labour force divided by the population aged 10 years and above.

Source: Various as above.

It may well be the case that the poor defined by consuming below a given poverty line, live on incomes earned by people who according to the hours worked criteria could hardly be considered under the category of under-employed in terms of hours spent in economic activity.

TABLE 3.2

Married Female Work Participation in Pakistan by Type of Survey: July-December 1979

Source of Information	Pakistan	Rural	Urban
Labour Force Survey	14.55	17.85	5.2
Migration Survey	2.72	2.43	2.56
Fertility Survey	11.40	12.60	8.20

Source: Irfan, Mohammad. "The determinants of female labour force participation" PIDE, PLM Research Report No.5, 1983.

3.4 The Project Commissioned Survey on Labour Force Measurment

In order to assess the sensitivity of recorded employment and unemployment information to different concepts of work, varying reference periods, and changing enumeration methodology, a pilot survey was commissioned from the Pakistan Federal Bureau of Statistics. The results of this survey were written up as a Project study (Irfan 1990).

TABLE 3.3

Underemployment and Job Dissatisfaction as Estimated by the National Manpower Commission (1974-87)

Years	Underemployed Persons (working less than 35 hours)		Employed Persons Looking for Second Job
1986-87	2282	3467	
	(10.00)		(12.08)
1985-86	2549	3471	
	(9.43)		(12.84)
1984-85	2486	3791	
	(9.22)	(14.06)	
1982-83	3248	—	
	(12.56)		—
1978-79	2907		—
	(12.47)		—
1974-75	857	—	
	(4.27)	—	

Source: National Manpower Commission, "A Strategy for Employment Promotion and Manpower Development in Pakistan (Interim Report)", p. 56, March 1988.

A sample of 1001 households in two rural (600 households) and two urban (401 households) locations were interviewed. The locations were purposively selected to offer a range of socio-economic and physical environments. There is every reason to expect that a conventional, narrow definition survey would have found Women's Labour Force Participation Rates (WLFPR), i.e proportion of women aged 10 or more who are measured as economically active, of between three (1981 Population Census result) and 12 per cent (mid-1980s Labour Force Survey results).

The 1001 households were interviewed during October-December 1989. The information collected pertained to 6345 persons out of which 41 per cent were in urban areas while the remaining were in rural areas. Roughly, 51 per cent of the information was gathered by the male enumerators while female enumerators collected 49 per cent of the responses. During the conduct of the survey, enumerators were instructed to distinguish between proxy and own responses.

The average size of the household in the rural sub-sample was 6.2 members, while in the urban areas, the average household consisted of 6.5 members. The economically active population per household after probing was estimated to be on average 2.1 and 2.2 persons respectively. The reported annual yearly income on the average for a rural household was Rs. 28,600 and for an urban household was reported to be Rs. 36,800 (the urban households were in areas designated as "middle income" by the Federal Bureau of Statistics).

Responses from those persons who claimed to be out of the labour force under the application of conventional conceptualisation of employment and unemployment, were then asked an additional question probing whether they were considered to be in any sense *"available for work"*. The result gave a significant increase in the labour force participation rates, irrespective of the reference period used as shown in Tables 3.4 and 3.5.

In comparison with the old definition, which does not include this question as an independent question, the labour force participation rate, particularly of the female respondents, shows a significant rise. The difference between these two participation rates, however, tends to narrow as the length of the reference period increases.

TABLE 3.4

Labour Force Participation Rate by Sex (Age 10+) by Reference Period and Measure of Labour Supply—1989

Reference Period	Old Definition			New Definition		
	Both Sexes	Male	Female	Both Sexes	Male	Female
1. One Week	45.1	69.5	19.6	50.2	71.9	27.6
2. One Day	44.9	68.4	20.3	50.0	71.0	28.2
3. One Month	46.0	69.2	21.9	50.7	71.5	29.0
4. Usual Status	45.7	69.7	20.6	48.5	70.7	25.4

Source: Irfan 1990.

It appears that the addition of this question *available for work* to other ques-tions envisaged to collect information on unemployment may be a regular feature for future data gathering exercises in Pakistan. It is therefore imperative to investigate in detail regarding the type of persons influenced by this addition and assess the meaning of such a change for policy formulation. The percentage distribution of those who were now recorded as unemployed due to the addition of this question shows that 96 per cent of the unemployment among women stems from this modification (see Table 3.6). In contrast, only 40 per cent of the unemployment among men can be ascribed to the additional probing.

TABLE 3.5

Labour Force Participation Rate by Sex/Reference Period and Measure of Labour Supply

Urban, Rural Irrigated and Rural Unirrigated (Age 10+)

Reference Period	Old Definition			New Definition		
	Both Sexes	Male	Female	Both Sexes	Male	Female
Urban						
1. One Week	42.4	68.3	13.5	49.0	71 7	23.1
2. One Day	40.6	65.8	12.6	47.9	70.0	22.6
3. One Month	44.1	67.5	18.1	49.3	71.2	24.2
4. Usual Status	45.3	70.5	17.2	47.3	70.3	20.9
Rural Irrigated						
1. One Week	47.0	72.4	21.2	50.8	73 7	27.4
2. One Day	47.5	71.8	22.6	51.4	73.4	29.0
3. One Month	48.1	72.2	23.5	51.4	73.3	29.1
4. Usual Status	46.5	71.3	21.2	49.2	72.7	25.2
Rural Unirrigated						
1. One Week	51.6	65 3	40.2	51 9	65.3	40.9
2. One Day	51.4	64 1	40.9	52.3	65.3	41.6
3. One Month	52.5	65.7	41.5	52.7	65.7	41.9
4. Usual Status	50.1	64.5	38.2	50.3	64.9	38.2

Source. Irfan 1990.

The incidence of unemployment among men in urban areas appears to have been influenced significantly (making 76 per cent addition) by the addition of this question. However, the effect on their counterparts in rural areas is less significant (26 per cent). One also finds a gradual diminution in the impact of this addition to the unemployment rate across successive levels of higher education of males. For instance, the effect of this definition dropped from 47 per cent on the illiterate to 30 per cent for matriculates and above. This appears to be enhanced in the case of rural areas. The effect of this modification in the definition of the female unemployment rate remains more or less uniform across different educational levels.

TABLE 3.6

Additional Unemployment due to Probing available for work (% of total unemployment by sex and education level)

Areas	Total	Illiterate	Pre-Matric	Matric & above
All Areas				
Male	40	47	37	30
Female	96	97	97	85
Both Sexes	71	79	68	47
Urban Areas				
Male	76	52	47	40
Female	97	98	98	92
Both Sexes	75	79	76	63
Rural Areas				
Male	26	41	13	15
Female	94	96	92	—
Both Sexes	65	80	47	15

Note: The difference in number unemployed yielded by new and old definitions on the basis of one week reference period as percentage of total unemployed under new definition are provided in this table.

The policy relevance of such a change in the statistical measurement is unclear. Can we regard these people who are defined as available for work while at the same time they are not seeking work as belonging to the same supply curve constituted by active job seekers? It is difficult to provide a definite answer. But the responses of those who reported themselves as available for work by the place at which they are available are relevant in this repect. As reflected by Table 3.7, nearly two-thirds of this specific group of unemployed would like to work within their own houses. The fraction is enlarged in the case of females wherein 87 per cent of the females would like to make themselves available for work if it is provided to them within their houses. Only two per cent of the females reported themselves for work anywhere in their district. One would have expected less resistance to mobility for the higher level of education. However, this is borne out only by men and not by women.

Table 3.8 shows the impact of probing to discover whether women declared as housewives did in fact undertake at least one hour of activity which could be classified as economic activity in terms of standard System of National Accounts classifications. The table shows a significant rise in the female economic activity rates particularly in rural areas. The number of females who can qualify as economically active once all their activities are reckoned rises by almost one

TABLE 3.7

Percentage Distribution of those available for Work by most distant Place at which available by Sex—All Areas

Place at which Available	All			Illiterate			Pre-matric			Matric +		
	Both Sexes	Male	Female	Both Sexes	Male	Female	Both Sexes	Male	Female	Both Sexes	Male	Female
1. Within this household	67	5	87	68	7	85	71	4	97	35	—	64
2. Within the Vill./Town	27	70	11	28	77	19	22	73	3	35	44	27
3. Anywhere in the District	3	9	2	—	—	—	3	9	—	20	33	9
4. Anywhere in this Province	1	5	—	1	4	—	1	5	—	5	11	—
5. Anywhere in this Country	2	11	—	2	22	—	3	9	—	5	12	—
%age of Sample	100	26	74	55	12	43	36	10	26	9	4	5

Source: Irfan 1990.

hundred per cent. The female labour force participation rate is very sensitive to the time cut-off point. If the cut-off point is set at 15 hours per week then the activity rate drops from 61 per cent to 36 per cent.

TABLE 3.8

Female Labour Force Participation

Areas	On the basis of weekly activities	On the weekly current status (new definition, including available for work)	On the weekly current status (old definition)
All Areas	46.68	27.6	19.6
Urban Areas	25.03	23.1	13.5
Rural Areas	61.44	29.2	25.8

Source: Irfan 1990.

The list of activities used, however, needs to be extended because roughly one quarter of the time spent by respondents in rural areas was recorded under the category of "other" or "unspecified". It needs to be emphasised that more detailed recording of activities requires application of care both in actual data collection as well as choice of the wordings which define an activity.

In the survey satisfactory fine tuning and sharp classification could not be achieved. For instance, under the care of animals was included feeding, grazing, milking animals, churning milk, collection of cow-dung and preparing dung cakes. The female labour force participation rate is sensitive to inclusion or exclusion of such border line cases. If care of animals as defined above is treated as non-economic, then the female activity rate drops by 20 per cent from 61 per cent to 46 per cent.

Indications of time underemployment in terms of hours and man-days is provided in Table 3.9. As revealed by the Table nearly 60 per cent of workers worked for 42 hours or more during the reference period. Those who worked less than 35 hours per week account for 29 per cent of the employed. The information on days worked during the year collected under the usual status approach shows that only 69 per cent of employed worked more than 240 days during the year. Only a small fraction (4%) of the employed were reported to have worked for 120 days or less.

In addition to application of an arbitrary norm for quantification of the under-employment, interpreting this estimated under employment as surplus labour in the sense available for work may be problematic too. The data collected for rural areas on cropwise time input highlights one of the problems faced in this respect as shown in Table 3.10.

If one were to apply conventional methods of data collection relying on the dichotomy of working/non-working then the resultant estimates of under-employment would indicate that half of the time of male and three fourths of that of female is unutilised. The results get substantially modified when non-economic

TABLE 3.9

Distribution of Hours and Days Economically Active

	Hours worked during a Week						Number of days worked during Year				
	<25 hours	25-34 hours	35-41 hours	42-48 hours	49-55 hours	>56 hours	Upto 60 days	61-120 days	120-180 days	181-240 days	241-365 days
Employer	17	8	—	17	8	50	—	—	—	6	94
Self-employed	14	10	10.8	16.8	11.8	36.6	1.9	2.1	3.8	19.7	72.4
Unpaid Family Helper	37.2	13.9	9.1	10.9	6.4	22.4	0.1	2.4	3.4	21.0	72.0
Employee	10.4	9.1	11.0	29.8	6.0	33.7	2.4	3.7	11.9	25.0	58.0
All	18.2	10.6	10.2	20.2	8.0	31.8	1.5	2.6	5.6	21.2	69.1

Source Irfan 1990.

activities performed by these workers are reckoned. As the last column of the table shows, only 11 per cent of women's time in Rabi can be identified as unutilised. This exercise therefore, underscores one of the major limitations of the procedures which tend to equate underemployment as time not in economic activity and a surplus of available labour time and energy for use elsewhere.

If planning and policy-making are to be well-informed then a more radical reform of data-collection methods is needed to bring other surveys closer into line with the Agricultural Census. A move towards collecting data in the form of time-budgets is needed to give greater understanding of the boundaries between fully active (economically and/or domestically), time genuinely inactive (i.e. with some weekly or seasonal slack time), and fully unemployed (with about forty hours a week or more time available for employment with/without strong locational restrictions). Rates of earnings for activities (and morbidity data to assess time and energy availability) would be also needed if a full understanding of underemployment in terms of time, productivity and availability is to be achieved.

TABLE 3.10

Percentage Distribution of Time Utilised and Unutilised in Rural Areas by Sex

Crop Time	Total Time	Economic Activity	Unutilised	Spent on Non-Economic Activity	Remaining Unutilised
Kharif					
Male	100	51	49	15	36
Female	100	25	75	54	21
Rabi					
Male	100	47	53	13	40
Female	100	24	76	65	11

Source: Irfan 1990.

A question was asked in the survey on work preferences by those declaring themselves unemployed. The responses cross-classified by urban/rural and by education level of the unemployed are shown in Table 3.11 and indicate strong preferences for government jobs by the educated (Matriculation and above), rural unemployed. In urban areas where the educated can hope to get jobs with private sector or engage in productive self-employment one finds a lower fraction of the educated expressing preferences for government job than their counterparts in rural areas.

The sample survey recorded 17 per cent of those with education level of matriculate and higher as unpaid family helpers. In response to one of the questions aimed at eliciting information on the level of satisfaction of these unpaid family helpers, as shown in Table 3.12, all of these unpaid helpers were satisfied with their current position in urban areas. A closer look at the data reveals that most of these unpaid family helpers (matric and above) were reported to be associated with the distribution businesses of the head of their households.

TABLE 3.11

Job Preference of the Unemployed by Sex/Education (Percentages)

	Total			Illiterate			Pre-Matric			Matric & above		
	Both Sexes	Male	Female	Both Sexes	Male	Female	Both Sexes	Male	Female	Both Sexes	Male	Female
1. Full Time with the Government												
(Rural)	21	40	5	5	15	—	28	35	17	88	86	100
(Urban)	13	25	4	10	23	2	7	15	—	40	53	25
2. Full Time paid with Private Sector												
(Rural)	11	17	5	9	15	6	17	29	—	6	7	—
(Urban)	17	39	—	12	29	—	25	56	—	7	13	—
3. Part Time Paid Employment												
(Rural)	14	3	24	18	4	26	10	6	17	—	—	—
(Urban)	17	11	21	15	6	21	17	13	21	18	13	25
4. Self-Employment												
(Rural)	2	—	5	4	—	6	—	—	—	—	—	—
(Urban)	8	1	14	12	—	19	8	3	12	—	—	—
5. Other Paid Work												
(Rural)	9	5	13	9	8	10	14	6	25	—	—	—
(Urban)	16	2	27	18	3	28	14	—	25	15	7	33
6. Work on Commission/Contract/Daily Wages												
(Rural)	42	34	50	54	58	52	31	23	41	6	7	—
(Urban)	29	22	34	33	39	30	29	13	42	15	13	17

Source. Irfan 1990

A striking contrast was provided by the information on rural unpaid family helpers in unirrigated areas, where all were not satisfied with their current status. Out of these nearly 62 per cent were actively looking for jobs. It must be mentioned, however, that they would not declare themselves as unemployed. The remainder who were not looking for jobs were not doing so primarily because of their belief that jobs were not available. Similarly, a very high percentage of unpaid family helpers of the 'educated' in irrigated areas of the rural sub-sample were not satisfied either and most of them were looking for jobs. A pressure towards rural-urban migration is clearly revealed.

TABLE 3.12

Unpaid Family Workers (Matric and above) by Level of Job Satisfaction by Rural/Urban (Percentages)

Area	Satisfied	Not Satisfied	Looking for job	Not Looking for job because believe it is not available
Urban Areas	100	—	—	—
Rural (Unirrigated)	—	100	62.5	37.5
Rural (Irrigated)	40	60	40.0	20.0
All Areas (% of unpaid Family workers of Matric and above)	59	41	27.0	14.0

Source: Irfan 1990.

The survey also indicated that proxy responses in general lead to under-reporting of the Labour Force Participation Rate. This is true in the case of urban areas and the irrigated sub-sample of rural areas both for male and female. In the case of the rural unirrigated sample, (20% of total sample), the female labour force participation rate is higher for proxy response than for self responses. A closer perusal of this sub-sample reveals that females up to the age of 39 reported lower labour force participation under self in comparison to proxy responses.

In the case of unemployment one gets similar differentials and they seem to be much more pronounced for women where proxy respondents tend to under-report. The gender of enumerator was found to have no significant effect.

In the case of declared 'students' only 4 to 5 per cent of the students reported participating in the labour market after probing. The majority of these worked as helpers in their family's enterprise. Similarly, children under the age of ten were not found to be significantly economically active. Thus it may be concluded that "housewife" is the only response into which further probing is generally desirable.

3.5 Conclusions

The present Labour Market Information System is a combination of data collection efforts made by various institutions in Pakistan with varying degrees of effectiveness. In order to improve the overall information system a thorough review is required of:

(a) *concepts:* aiming at better representation of actual conditions in Pakistan and moving away from dichotomies (including the large-scale/small-scale dichotomy) towards more meaningful finer gradations, possibly using time budget data and more probing questionnaires and interview techniques in gauging economic activity. Labour demand and supply side surveys, population censuses and Household Income and Expenditure Surveys should use identical categorisations, including the choice of reference period. Attitudinal questions have a role to play in indicating the dynamics in the labour market and likely policy responses;
(b) *sampling:* aiming at more rigorous sampling design with genuine censuses (not mailed questionnaires), or larger samples, finer- mesh stratification or purposive sampling to ensure adequate representation of policy-significant groups, e.g. women-headed households;
(c) *regularity:* aiming at intervals between surveys which are meaningful for policy purposes, generally annual surveys are unnecessary and a period of two or three years is necessary and sufficient, though India works on a basis of five years;
(d) *timeliness:* aiming at all survey data becoming available to policy makers within two years of the start of data collection.

The Federal Bureau of Statistics lies at the apex of the statistical system in Pakistan. Major data gathering exercises such as Population Censuses and Agricultural Censuses are conducted by two of its wings, while the Labour Force Survey and Household Income and Expenditure surveys are conducted by the Bureau itself.

The Federal Bureau of Statistics plays also a supervisory and coordinating role. For instance, the Provincial Bureaux of Statistics collect data for the Census of Manufacturing Industry (CMI) on large scale manufacturing industries which are compiled together for the country level by the Federal Bureau of Statistics.

The Provincial Labour Directorates are vital sources of data on parts of the labour market. Annual Establishment Enquiries, occasional district surveys, information from employment exchanges and all the data collected for assessing the implementation of labour laws is done by the Provincial Labour Directorates. But the Federal Bureau of Statistics would clearly be the lead agency in any review of the survey aspects of the Labour Market Information System.

Surveys conducted by academic institutions tend to suggest that there is a good deal of reluctance on the part of the establishments and employers to part with accurate information, particularly to official enumerators, while they were more willing to give more accurate responses to research organisations. Depending upon acceptable financial arrangements, experiments in commissioning non-government agencies to undertake surveys of the labour market, including wages and incomes rates monitoring, could be undertaken in more sensitive areas with conventional anonymity conditions.

CHAPTER 4

The Frontiers to Employment Generation and the Need for Training in Large Scale Units in the 1990s

4.1 Introduction

State planning since the creation of Pakistan has been primarily concerned with the development of larger scale employment units. Such units were seen as efficient and the mainspring of economic growth and prosperity, while smaller scale units were seen as performing a holding role until the larger scale units grew sufficiently to displace them and employ their labour more productively (see Kibria 1984 and 1990). It must also be said that the controllers of larger units in the public and private sectors were well positioned to make the case for their prioritisation politically.

The labour market information system (as shown in Chapter 3 of this Report), macro-economic policy (as shown in Chapter 2 of this Report), and the whole framework of state assistance and regulation have been oriented towards larger scale units, leaving smaller scale units invisible, unassisted, unregulated and in those senses "informal". But whether smaller scale units are universally "informal" in the economic and technical senses of not offering regular wage employment and being unmechanised, is a question to be examined in the next chapter.

In this chapter, we seek to examine the likely frontiers to employment generation by larger scale units in the 1990s. There are conflicting demands on large scale units in the 1990s, and employment generation needs to be seen as only one of those demands which must establish its claim for prioritisation in competition with other claims. If large scale units will naturally, or can be cost-effectively, encouraged to generate significant amounts of new employment then the need to undergo the complex process of reorienting state planning towards enabling myriads of small-scale employment initiatives will be reduced.

4.2 The Prospects for Employment Generation in Large Scale Agriculture and Manufacturing

As indicated in Section 1, the National Manpower Commission places little demand on large scale agriculture and manufacturing to generate significant amounts of new employment in the 1990s. Removal of actual subsidies to mechanisation and limited state Research and Development "seed" money to shifting sectoral compositions to more labour intensive activities are anticipated to be necessary and sufficient to generate the additional, unquantified employment that larger scale units can be reasonably expected to generate.

The National Manpower Commission gives greater stress to natural and human resource development by larger scale units and to that extent absolves them from employment generation as an over-riding priority.

Hussain in his study on rural employment (Hussain 1990) concludes that, even with a considerable slowing in mechanisation, agriculture (large and small scale) will only absorb about 30 per cent of the growth in the rural labour force in the 1990s (see Table 4.1). His calculations arise from extrapolations of past technical performance into the future assuming labour will be absorbed at subsistence incomes (Farm Households in the Table means all households deriving subsistence from agriculture). We will examine here whether such an extrapolation can be justified for agriculture as a whole and the dominant large scale units in particular.

TABLE 4.1

Estimated Changes in Labour Absorption in Crop Production during 1988-2000

(in million)

	Policy 1	Policy 2
1. Increase in Labour Demand (Man days per year)	292.291	361.987
2. Man Days of Production Labour Required to Sustain one Farm Household	225.11	225 11
3. Increase in Absorption of Farm Households	1.297	1.604
4. Increase in Absorption of Farm Population	8.431	10.426

Note: (1) Estimates Hussain

Sources: (i) WAPDA XAES data on Coefficients (Unpublished), (ii) Pakistan Census of Agriculture, 1972, 1980, (iii) Report of the Farm Mechanisation Committee, Ministry of Agriculture and Works, Government of Pakistan, 1970, (iv) Pakistan Census of Agriculture Machinery

Note: Policy 1 (a) Growth of tractors and size of tractors in the period 1988-2000 remains the same as in the period 1968-1975

(b) Introduction of mechanised harvesting does not cover more than 10 percent of the total cultivated area

(c) ncrease in delivery and application efficiencies of irrigation resulting in a growth rate of crop production of 3 7 per cent per year, with associated increases in cropping intensities

Policy 2 (a) Growth rate of tractors during 1988-2000, slows down to half the rate observed in the period 1968-1975

(b) Same as in Policy 1

(c) Same as in Policy 1

Source of Table: Hussain 1990

Data from Agricultural Censuses as well as Labour Force Surveys are suggestive of a lower growth rate of employment in agriculture compared to non-agriculture sectors in the rural areas. This performance of the agricultural sector has been attributed to mechanisation, particularly tractorisation, and changes in the farm size distribution.

Farm size distribution is discussed by Hussain, who arrives at the conclusion that some tenancy arrangements will continue despite tendencies of larger scale farming to ensure tied supplies of seasonal labour for large landowners. Thus small scale holdings appear to be surviving. But this survival will depend on relationships of production in agriculture which will remain complex with varying degrees of labour intensity of land use co-existing on terms arranged to suit large landowners. To separate large scale and small scale agriculture for policy purposes and attempt to encourage small scale, more labour intensive farming would show a grave misunderstanding of the underlying situation. Only if the small scale farmers were genuinely independent farmers would such an approach be likely to succeed. The dynamics of agriculture will depend upon the priorities of large scale unit profitability.

The impact of the three land reforms has been quite limited as far as the farm size distribution is concerned. The Gini coefficient as a measure of inequality in terms of the crop area actually rose from 0.593 in 1960 to 0.611 in 1980. A comparison between the Agriculture Censuses of 1972 and 1980 indicates that both number and area under the size categories of 7.5 acres and less rose over time in relative as well as in absolute terms. The other size categories in general experienced a decline.

Inheritance custom and law requiring sub-division of land among the heirs in conjunction with growing population means a rise over time in the relative share of small farms which is understandable. What probably needs an explanation is the resiliency of large farms not only to retain but increase the average size of the farm (operational holdings) though with some decline in its relative share in the total. There is a general consensus among researchers that this phenomenon is due to resumption of land by large land owners from tenants. This is also visible from a comparison of the Agricultural Census of 1972 with that of 1980 wherein both the number and area of tenant operated farms has declined.

A rise in the average size of the farm at the top and bottom size categories of owner-operated farms is also visible. However, it is difficult to exactly identify the factors underlying this distribution pattern due to non-availability of adequate data. The information contained in the Agriculture Census is of limited value. For instance, farm area reported in the 1980 Census is roughly five per cent less than that in the 1972 Agriculture Census. Unless the distribution pattern of this difference which is around two million acres is reckoned it is difficult to have conclusive evidence on the inter-temporal changes in the farm size distribution. It must not be forgotten that the data in the Agriculture Census pertained to the operational holdings and not to ownership. Increase in the average size of farm at the top of the distribution can occur by either of two processes: (i) resumption of land from tenants by owners, and (ii) development of joint ventures or informal tenancy. While the former process has been widely discussed and highlighted, the latter, which would be consistent with the Hussain view, has been hardly mentioned.

As mentioned in Chapter 1, there have been a number of studies which deal with the impact of tractorisation on labour use in agriculture. One set of studies claimed and provided evidence pertaining to the labour displacement effect of tractors while the other set of studies argued that the direct labour displacement effect has been more than counter-balanced by the indirect output increasing effect of the tractors. As mentioned in Chapter 1, a survey comparing 1976-77 and 1983-84 found that labour use per cultivated acre declined during this period by about six per cent. This study, however, failed to provide a cogent explanation of the decline in labour use during this period even on the farm using bullocks. At best the available evidence regarding the effect of tractors on labour use can be regarded as inconclusive but certainly there is no evidence of increasing employment per unit area.

It must be added that since the late 1970s, mechanisation in agriculture experienced additional impetus through the introduction of imported harvesters and threshers. The extensive use of combine harvesters and mechanical cotton pickers appears to be in the offing. There is no doubt that introduction of these machines on a large scale will have an adverse repercussion for labour use.

A combine harvester for instance, on average harvests and threshes the produce from three acres in one hour which is equivalent to 21 days manual labour. If mechanical cotton pickers and combine harvesters are introduced on the scale of tractors, then it is seasonal wage labour for women that may suffer most pushing rural landless households deeper into poverty vulnerability.

There is an argument that, through land redistribution and reversing mechanisation, many more of the growing rural labour force could be absorbed productively into agriculture. This question was addressed in Irfan and Arif (1985). This exercise was aimed at assessing the extent to which the available land resources under the current distribution pattern and productivity conditions can absorb the farm population. The following assumptions were made in this exercise (similar to those made in Hussain 1990):

(a) The farm population receives income only through crop and livestock (non-farm labour or ex-village labour participation is not allowed);

(b) A subsistence income consistent with nutritional needs of 2550 calories per adult was used to define an income requirement. This was translated into a required crop area of 6.2 acres on average for owner operators. In the case of owner-come-tenant, the required farm area was 9.3 and for tenants it was 12.4 acres;

(c) It was assumed that people can move only within districts, in other words the district was chosen as the unit of analysis.

In order to deal with inter-district productivity differentials, the per acre productivity of each district was used as an index to adjust the required area for subsistence in that district. Any aggregate insufficiency of land resources to yield subsistence income was identified as generating landless households. Around two-thirds of the agriculturally-dependent population using this procedure was identified as landless. Table 4.2 provides the details at provincial level.

Table 4.2 shows that nearly two-thirds of "farm" households cannot meet their subsistence needs from existing land resources. Incipient "landlessness",

TABLE 4.2

Estimated Landless 1980

(% of Farm Households)

Near Landless Provinces	Owner	Owner/ Tenant	Tenant	All	Pure Landless	Total
Pakistan	60.6	52.6	72.2	62.0	5.1	67.1
Punjab	60.2	55.4	70.9	61.7	6.3	68.0
Sind	33.5	20.7	71.1	49.3	3.2	52.5
N.W.F.P.	83.5	61.5	80.3	79.6	2.4	82.0
Baluchistan	67.8	71.2	94.0	72.1	2.8	74.8

Source: M. Irfan, "Population Growth and its Implications for Socio-Economic Development", Pakistan Institute of Development Economics, Islamabad (unpublished Mimeograph), 1988.

thus defined, is highest in NWFP (82%) and lowest (52%) in Sind province. In terms of numbers, 2.7 million agriculture-dependent households in 1980 would not have land sufficient enough to earn subsistence income.

The paper concludes that only under extreme circumstances entailing radical departures from the past, might the existing land have afforded a subsistence income to all the *farm population*. These measures should include redistributional land reforms with a permissible upper ceiling of 25 acres for a household, abolition of tenancy, transmigration of farm population from land short to land surplus districts and above all improving the per acre productivity in Barani and less productive districts to the average of the country. Even if the political will existed to introduce these radical land distributive changes, the required increase in the productivity levels of the agriculture sector in the less productive districts will not prove to be an easy or costless task.

The finding of the above exercise highlights the growing physical and socio-political imbalance between the land resources and population as well as making it very clear that any thoughts of absorbing a growing rural population within small scale agriculture are not very realistic and that a drive for productivity gains per worker and per unit area are the current requirement.

The conclusions of the National Commission on Agriculture to this effect are well-based, though the Commission's recommendations are still very demanding in terms of aggregate investment requirements. In order to implement even the National Manpower Commission's limited recommendations, which appear to accept the existing farm size distribution and the dominance of agriculture by larger scale farms, the needed investment in infrastructure and set of policies which will facilitate the achievement of the Commission's limited objectives are likely to be large and need the surpluses that efficient large scale agriculture produces.

It is a matter of conventional wisdom that larger scale manufacturing in Pakistan is more mechanised on the basis of imported machinery than can be warranted by the relative availability of labour compared to availability of foreign exchange. As outlined in Chapter 1, much of the blame for this situation has been put on the impact of government policies on the relative factor price of local labour and imported machinery.

Comparisons between large and small scale establishments by industrial sub-sectors made by Wizarat and Zafar show that, in the early 1980s, large scale establishments did have significantly higher capital per worker (though not generally the quoted multiple of eighty). Table 4.3 shows that large scale units also paid those workers significantly higher wage rates when taking industry sub-sector by sub- sector (Wizarat and Zafar 1989). Part of the difference between large scale and small scale units probably lies in the different product mixes of the two sub-sectors and differential real wage rates.

TABLE 4.3

Ratio of the Small Scale Sector Wage Rate to the Large Scale Sector Wage Rate 1980

Interval of relative Wage Rate	Number of Industries	
	1976/77	1983/84
0.00 - 0.20	10 (16)	18 (29)
0.20 - 0.40	31 (50)	29 (47)
0.40 - 0.60	13 (21)	9 (15)
0.60 - 0.80	5 (8)	1 (2)
0.80 - 1.00	1 (2)	3 (5)
1.00 - 1.50	0 (0)	0 (0)
1.50 - 2.00	1 (2)	0.(0)
2.00 and above	0 (0)	1 (2)
Total	62 (100)	62 (100)

Percentages in parenthesis.

Sources. CMI 1976/77, CMI 1982/83, SHMI 1976/77, SHMI 1983/84; in Wizarat and Zafar, 1989.

The Systems (Pvt.) Ltd survey (1990) asked larger scale units' managements their reasons for installing new machinery (see Table 4.4). The most commonly given "most important" reason was to increase production followed by improving quality, substituting machinery for labour hardly figured at all. Efficient, higher quality growth is perceived as requiring up-to-date machinery.

Ex post, it may be true that these perceptions may not be realised as indicated by the findings of Wizarat and Zafar (see Table 4.5) that, while labour productivity rose greatly between 1955 and 1981, total factor productivity including capital and labour actually tended to fall. This suggests that introduction of machinery was being pushed beyond the frontier of economic rationality in practice. But a more likely explanation is that labour use is being increasingly underestimated in the large unit sub-sector.

TABLE 4.4

Reasons for Installation of New Machinery

Reasons	Number of Respones				Percentages			
	Most Imp.	V. Imp.	Imp.	Total Imp.	Most	V. Imp.	Imp.	Total
Sind								
1	2.0	0.0	2.0	4.0	5.0	0.0	6.0	3.0
2	0.0	0.0	1.0	1.0	0.0	0.0	3.0	0.0
3	8.0	8.0	8.0	14.0	20.0	22.0	24.0	22.0
4	3.0	10.0	12.0	25.0	7.0	28.0	36.0	23.0
5	23.0	13.0	2.0	38.0	58.0	37. 0	6.0	35.0
6	0.0	0.0	2.0	2.0	0.0	0.0	6.0	1.0
7	0.0	0.0	0.0	0.0	0.0	0.0	0.0	0.0
8	3.0	4.0	6.0	13.0	7.0	11.0	18.0	12.0
Punjab								
1	0.0	0.0	2.0	2.0	0.0	0.0	8.0	2.0
2	0.0	0.0	0.0	0.0	0.0	0.0	0.0	0.0
3	12.0	14.0	5.0	31.0	34.0	42.0	21.0	34.0
4	3.0	10.0	12.0	25.0	8.0	30.0	52.0	27.0
5	20.0	8.0	4.0	32.0	57.0	24.0	17.0	35.0
6	0.0	0.0	0.0	0.0	0.0	0.0	0.0	0.0
7	0.0	0.0	0.0	0.0	0.0	0.0	0.0	0.0
8	0.0	1.0	0.0	1.0	0.0	3.0	0.0	1.0
Country Totals								
1	2.0	0.0	4.0	6.0	2.0	0.0	7.0	3.0
2	0.0	0.0	1.0	1.0	0.0	1.0	1.0	0.0
3	20.0	22.0	13.0	55.0	27.0	32.0	23.0	27.0
4	6.0	20.0	24.0	50.0	8.0	29.0	42.0	25.0
5	43.0	21.0	6.0	70.0	58.0	30.0	10.0	35.0
6	0.0	0.0	2.0	2.0	0.0	0.0	3.0	1.0
7	0.0	0.0	0.0	0.0	0.0	0.0	0.0	0.0
8	3.0	5.0	6.0	14.0	4.0	7.0	10.0	7.0

Source: Systems (Pvt) Ltd, 1990.

Reason Codes:

1. To reduce regular employees.
2. To reduce irregular employees.
3. To improve quality.
4. To reduce cost.
5. To increase production.
6. To avoid labour union.
7. To avoid government labour laws.
8. Others.

However, if in the 1980s there has been a growing recognition by management of large scale manufacturing units that mechanisation alone is not enough to guarantee increased profitability, then two types of response would have been rational. Firstly, to reduce unit costs by opting for greater labour intensity in real terms and hiring more workers for each machine and working the machines more efficiently, harder and/or longer. Secondly, to seek to reduce labour costs per machine hour in pecuniary terms by exerting downward pressure on wage rates. There is not much evidence of the first response (power/energy availability is a frequent constraint found by the Systems (Pvt.) Ltd. survey), but much evidence of the second in terms of casualising and contracting labour. Tables 4.6 and 4.7 from the Systems (Pvt.) Ltd. survey show a widespread prevalence of "irregular/ contract" labour working 26 or 27 days per month for a monthly "household subsistence" income from that employment of around Rs 1,000.

It is hard to see how wages could be depressed further to encourage greater labour use and the implications of raising the costs of imported and domestically manufactured machinery are likely to be less output, lower quality, fewer units, and hence higher unit costs and less employment.

Also, if the argument is accepted that actual employment in larger scale units is currently underestimated in the Census of Manufacturing Industry by about the one-third indicated in the Systems (pvt) Ltd survey, then the conclusions and recommendations on not forcing up employment in large scale units of the National Manpower Commission make even greater sense. But the argument depends crucially on the view that the actual size of the labour force in large-scale manufacturing has always been underestimated and has been increasingly underestimated during the 1980s by the Censuses of Manufacturing Industry.

TABLE 4.5

Compound Annual Rates of Growth of the Value Added Index, the Aggregate Input Index and the Total Factor Productivity Index for Large Scale Manufacturing 1955-1981

Tear	Value-added Index	Aggregate Input index	Total Factor Productivity Index
1955-56 to 1959-60	17.45	18.09	– 0.54
1962-63 to 1969-70	10.19	9.72	0.54
1970-71 to 1980-81	5.84	7.89	–2.00
1955-56 to 1980-81	12.77	13.03	– 0.23

Source : Wizarat and Zafar 1989.

Overall, it seems likely that mechanisation is more deeply integrated into the structure of larger scale manufacturing than as a mere response to relative factor pricing. If this is accepted, then it can be argued that larger scale manufacturing units not only employ significantly more people per unit of fixed capital and output than conventional wisdom conceived, but are also attempting to reduce unit costs primarily by reducing wage rates, not employment or mechanisation.

TABLE 4.6

Number of Firms Using Irregular/Contract Workers by Industry

Industrial Sub-Sector	No. of Firms	Percentage of Firms			
		Reg. Only	Reg. With Irr.	Reg. With Cont.	Reg. With Irr./Cont.
Textiles	57	0	68	53	21
Mechanical Eng. Transport	33	3	58	48	9
Food, Beverage,	29	0	62	62	24
Tobacco Chemical, Chemical Prod.	11	0	73	55	27
Non Metallic Products	11	0	91	45	36
Leather, Rubber	8	0	88	38	25
Footwear, Apparel	5	0	100	20	20
Other	8	0	75	50	25
Totals	162	1	69	51	21

Source : Systems (Pvt) Ltd., 1990.

As wage rates are reduced, machines are still seen as the best way of disciplining low paid, low motivated, often illiterate labour into maintaining output to a minimal quality standard. The large scale manufacturing sector can then be seen in 1990 not only to be the pampered child of government patronage of earlier periods, but also stuck in a low output quality, low labour quality, low wage trap using a rational amount of mechanisation. A trap which could spring disastrously as exposure increases to international competition based on very different principles of organisation.

The National Manpower Commission instincts then find a rational, supporting argument here that the basic problem in large scale manufacturing in Pakistan in the 1990s is a human resource development problem not a factor price or employment problem. Imposing a priority of increasing employment on this fragile structure would be inappropriate and dangerous. The need at this time is to break through into higher output quality, higher labour quality (and appropriately higher wage rates), and internationally competitive costs, not merely to increase numbers of people measured as being employed in the notoriously inaccurate Census of Manufacturing Industry.

Getting the price of machinery right and then letting market forces work is hardly relevant to this task. A state-enabled revolution in skill and occupational training and managerial attitudes and behaviour towards skilled workers is needed, which the National Manpower Commission recommendations on training do move towards. Machines and workers need to be understood as complementing each other with workers in control of the process, and neither as being in competition with each other, nor as machines dictating to workers the pace and form of work.

TABLE 4.7

Average Income of Irregular/Contract Workers

Industry	Respon-dents	Averages			
		Daily Wage	No. of Days	Monthly	House-hold
Sind					
Textiles	42.0	56.0	26.0	1481.0	1175.0
Mechanical Eng. Transport	26.0	42.0	25.0	1186.0	923.0
Food, Beverage, Tobacco	17.0	28.0	26.0	760.0	884.0
Chemical, Chemical Prod.	8.0	36.0	26.0	971.0	2761.0
Non Metalic Products	15.0	32.0	26.0	858.0	1394.0
Leather, Rubber	2.0	30.0	26.0	780.0	2955.0
Footwear, Apparel	4.0	41.0	26.0	1079.0	1767.0
Other	7.0	42.0	26.0	1180.0	1582.0
Totals	121.0	43.0	26.0	1163.0	1285.0
Punjab					
Textiles	54.0	41.0	29.0	1166.0	1389.0
Mechanical Eng. Transport	34.0	30.00	25.0	813.0	1523.0
Food, Beverage, Tobacco	31.0	33.0	25.0	930.0	1354.0
Chemical, Chemical Prod	10.0	31.00	26.0	886.0	1697.0
Non Metallic Products	4.0	32.0	25.0	1075.0	575.0
Leather, Rubber	10.0	34.0	25.0	1137.0	1229.0
Footwear, Apparel	4.0	32.0	25.0	875.0	1287.0
Other	6.0	28.0	26.0	850.0	850.0
Totals	153.0	35.0	27.0	997.0	1377.0

Source: Project Survey of Employment in Large Scale Manufacturing

4.3 The Public Sector and Employment Generation

The public sector in Pakistan has been a continuing source of employment expansion since the creation of the state in 1947. Table 4.8 indicates that since 1966, the number of civil servants in Federal government (that is generally workers without significant line service delivery functions) has grown one and a half times. The first half of the 1980s saw almost as many new posts created as were needed to run the whole Federal administration in 1966. There were significantly more Federal civil servants per head of population in 1986 than 1966.

Between 1983 and 1988, across the whole public sector, Table 4.9 shows most types of public sector employment growing faster than the overall labour force (one of the apparent exceptions is the Federal government service, which is surprising given that table 4.8 drawn from the same report suggested a 22 per cent increase between 1983 and 1986 alone).

TABLE 4.8

Civil Servants in Pakistan

Census	Number of Civil Servants	%age change over (1966)
1966	74.664	—
1970	83,047	11.25
1973	86,939	16.47
1977	111,692	49.63
1980	121,153	62.30
1983	153,144	105.11
1986	187,925	151.69

Source· Census of Employees of Federal Government (Different years) in *Public Sector Employment,* National Manpower Commission Study No.6, 1989.

There is great scepticism, often expressed as outright cynicism, about the contributions of this expanded public sector to the production efforts of Pakistan. However, such debates have now been overtaken by the structural reality that the fiscal situation cannot support further expansion. Annual fiscal deficits of between five and ten percent of GNP are already demanding a radical review of the whole taxation system to finance existing imbalances.

The National Manpower Commission sees a necessity for public sector employment expansion in the line delivery of human resource development services. In primary education and primary health care, especially in rural areas, there is seen to be an immediate need to train and deploy thousands of additional workers. However, the Commission does not present proposals for financing this expansion.

While such recommendations merit sympathetic consideration and may merit prioritisation above many other claims on government resources on grounds of meeting basic needs and cost-effective human resource development, there are risks in the present conjuncture of undertaking a crash programme:

(a) a crash programme will require training facilities to be set up for a short period and then to be run down, involving both start-up and close-down costs probably within a decade (there is a parallel element in the expansion of doctor's training in the 1970s);

(b) a crash programme in expanding public sector employment will do nothing to lower expectations of a right to public sector employment on achieving Matriculation;

(c) a crash programme not supported by budgets to equip and maintain employees adequately in the field will be quickly discredited.

The Commission does advocate that new training for rural schools and health posts be undertaken in the rural areas which might reduce costs and ensure greater commitment. But the above risks are still present. Any expansion of the public sector in present circumstances is bound to be seen and probably treated, opportunistically by "gate-keepers" to public employment. Certainly, planning the training of public sector service delivery workers at a rate significantly greater than the rate of population growth is totally justified, but criteria of sustainability, cost- effectiveness, and likely impact on those selected/those not selected/and ultimate beneficiaries would militate against a crash programme.

TABLE 4.9

Public Employment - Average Annual Growth Rate (1983-88)

	Government Bodies	Autonomous Govt.	Local
Federal	2.48	5.58	—
Punjab	9.66	4.89 *	3.99
Sind	7.80	2.50	5.29
Baluchistan	10.35	185.72	—

* Growth rate pertains to 1985-88.

Source: Public Sector Employment, National Manpower Commission Study No.6, 1989.

4.4 Human Resource Skill Development as a Joint Responsibility of Government and Larger Scale Employing Units

Table 4.10 summarises the overall education and training system as it stood in 1988/89. The figures suggest that just over eleven million people were in educational institutions in Pakistan. There were around fifty million people aged between six and twenty years of age in Pakistan at that time. There is much room for raising the proportion of young people in all formal education and training.

The balance between levels and forms of education and training in Table 4.10 suggest that vocational training is still a major lagging sector despite its impressive 8.2 per cent annual enrollment growth rate between 1978/79 and 1988/89. The process by which in the past more doctors than nurses were trained in Pakistan may well not be unique in terms of disproportionately small numbers of technical support workers compared to numbers of professional workers.

Estimates of the total annual output of skilled and semi-skilled workers are shown in Tables 4.11 and 4.12. Around 75,000 of this annual output of such workers have received formal training. Given around 15,00,000 people enter the workforce each year this accounts for 1 in 20 of the new entrants. Lee reports that SouthKorea is currently graduating about 2,75,000 formally vocationally trained people a year out of about 6,00,000 entrants to the workforce (Lee 1990).

For a cross-section of skilled worker trades, an estimated annual deficiency in 1984 is shown in Table 4.13. Formal training appeared to be catering for less than one in seven of the numbers required in those trades. An annual enrollment growth rate of 8.2 per cent in those trades allowing for demand increasing at the rate of population growth would mean that, in 1990, formal training would be accounting for about one in five of the numbers required but the absolute gap in terms of numbers would actually have grown. It is therefore appropriate that the

Seventh Plan allocations show the largest planned proportional increase, as shown in Table 4.14.

TABLE 4.10

Number and Enrolment in Education Institutions by kind in Pakistan 1988-89

	Educational Institutions		Annual Growth Rate in Enrolment, 1978-79 to 1988-89 (%)
	Number	Enrolment (000)	
Primary Schools	87,545	7,768	4.2
Middle Schools	6,560	2,216	5.5
High Schools	5,183	715	4.1
Sec Vocational Institutions	235	64	8.2
Arts and Science Colleges	599	439	6.5
Professional Colleges	99	80	1.8
Universities	22	69	6.0

Source: Mix of General/Vocational Educational Development in Pakistan, National Manpower Commission, 1989.

TABLE 4.11

Supply of Skilled Workers, 1989

Programme	Annual Output
(a) Output from the 37 institutions which comprise the National Vocational Training Project (NVTP)—Two shift operation.	12584
(b) Output from 7 institutions of the Punjab Government outside the NVTP—One shift Operation.	1250
(c) Establishment of 21 new VTCs in rural and sub-urban areas	2200
(d) Apprenticeship Programme being administered in about 454 establishments	
(e) Programmes being administered by various establishments outside the Apprenticeship Programmes (viz Pakistan Steel Mill, Railways, PIA, Shipyard and Karachi Port Trust).	4000
(f) Informal Training under the Ustad-Shagird System (No data is available regarding this form of training, output being quoted is therefore only an estimate	20000
Total	39334

Source: Skill Development in the Manufacturing Sector, National Manpower Commission, 1989

TABLE 4.12

Supply of Semi-Skilled Workers, 1989

Programme		Annual Output
(i)	Output from Centres of Provincial Small Industries Corporations/Boards. There are a total of 378 such centres imparting training in the Engineering, Leather, Carpet and Handicraft areas.	7000
(ii)	Output from OPF Training Institutions (Polytrade Schools).	2500
(iii)	Output from 16 institutions of the Punjab Agency for Barani Areas Development.	2500
(iv)	Output of 4 urban and 17 village workshop.	4000
(v)	Output from 500 private institutions. Some details from the 150 accredited institutions only are available no details of the remaining institutions are available. Indicated output figures are an estimate.	20000
(vi)	Output from about 15 Polytechnics/Colleges of Technology through their evening extension programmes	3000
(vii)	Output from Ustad-Shagird System. No data is available regarding form of training, indicated output figures are an estimate	
	Total:	59000

Source: Skill Development in the Manufacturing Sector, National Manpower Commission, 1989.

But the questions raised in the National Manpower Commission reports:

Skill Development and Productive Employment Manufacturing Sector (NMC Committee No. 1, 1989),

Mix of General/Vocational Educational Development in Pakistan (NMC Committee No.4, 1989),

Women's Employment and Training (NMC Committee No. 8, 1989), and four other recent surveys (Kazi 1990, Kemal 1990, Lee 1990, and EmmayAssociates 1991) are not so much about the quantity of formal technical and vocational education and training, but about the qualitative approach to such education and training.

From the supply side, Lee's study reports very little communication with potential employers of technical and vocational education graduates and some problems in placements (Lee 1990). On the demand side, Kemal's study reports middle-level technical worker shortages but low levels of satisfaction of employers with the skills of current graduates (Kemal 1990).

The National Manpower Commission is very clear that the way forward is to break with the past practice of designing training in relative isolation and abstraction and implementing it without built-in workplace experience. Potential employers should be involved in design and implementation and public sector funding should be available for private initiatives and the private sector should be involved in funding public sector-based training. In effect, the boundary between public and private sectors and between training and work should be dissolved.

TABLE 4.13

Annual Requirement of Skilled Workers and Output of Training Institutions in 1984

Trades	6th Plan Requirement	Out of Training Institutions	Approximate Gap
Blacksmiths	5,050	5	5,045
Auto Mechanic	918	530	388
Electrician	6,249	3,732	2,517
Machinist	1,596	1,006	590
Plumber	744	129	615
Painter	2,552	102	2,450
Mason	16,791	125	16,666
Carpenter	14,510	568	13,942
Welder	3,729	1,007	2,722
Fitters & Mechanics	14,965	4,923	10,042
Driver	22,334	71	22,263
Moulder	337	21	316
Total	89,775	12,219	77,556

Source: ILO-ARTEP (1987, Vol.V) in Amjad (ed) 1989.

Thus the major role allotted to larger scale employing units in the 1990s by the National Manpower Commission is human resource development rather than increasing the numbers of people directly employed.

The 1991 report by Emmay Associates (Emmay Associates1991) arrives at similar strong conclusions on the current failings of the present technical/vocational education and training system from the perspectives of training centres' Principals, pass-outs and pass-out employers—conclusions similar to those of recent Asian Development Bank and World Bank studies. Principals feel under-resourced, pass-outs have as much difficulty as degree graduates in finding employment (wage or self) or further training, and employers find pass-outs ill-equipped for the realities of work-places.

As even large scale employing units have adopted strategies of using cheap workers with low literacy and other skills to produce low quality output at a machine paced rate, the marginal cost of instituting more formal training will appear high to individual employers, who to date have been willing to "free-ride" on others' training rather than introduce their own schemes (Emmay Associates, 1991, 209). Therefore, an enabling government approach will require new resources to "seed" initiatives. Targeting on large scale employers, including those in the public sector itself, will mean both opportunities of increasing returns to scale and joint funding as envisaged.

TABLE 4.14

Summary of Seventh Plan Allocations for Various Sub-Sectors of Education

(Rupees Million)

	Sixth Plan		Seventh Plan
	Allocation	Expenditure	Allocation
1. Primary Education	7,000	3,533	10,128
2. Secondary	4,125	3,843	6,404
3. Teacher Education	305	182	287
4. Technical Education	1,315	900	2,000
5. College Education	1,300	1,233	615
6. Scholarship	660	739	760
7. Literacy & Mass Education	750	834	300
8. University Education	2,100	1,383	1,800
9. Library System	455	125	86
10. Misc. Programmes	570	395	150
11. Other Divisions	250	263	150
Total	18,830	13,430	22,680

Note: The Sixth Plan allocation and expenditure are at current prices as against the Seventh Plan allocations which are at 1987-88 prices.

Source: Seventh Five Year Plan, 1988-93, Planning Commission, Government of Pakistan, undated.

The need for net public sector funding for training can also be reduced through revenue generation by the training institutions themselves, if feasible and appropriate. Sales of output and marketing services would not only raise revenue but also educate trainees in marketing awareness (Emmay Associates, 1991, 217). The National Manpower Commission also sees the principle of greater market accountability as applicable to the development of Research and Development capabilities in science and technology in Universities through the seeking of commissioned research from the private sector and rights to retain material rewards from such research (Meeting Pakistan Manpower's Needs in Science and Technology for the Twentieth and Twenty First Centuries, NMC Committee No.8, 1989).

But all such initiatives in training and research and development at every level will require much more sensitive handling of the tension between local, practical accountability to existing enterprises and national, abstract certification/ recognition. In the past, the latter aspect has received too much attention and the balance needs to be altered.

4.5 Access for Women and Young People to Employment in Larger Scale Employing Units

The principle, also advocated by the National Manpower Commission, of stressing human resource development in the technical/vocational skills area as a joint responsibility of government and larger employing units is clearly in the spirit of an enabling government. However, that principle, if applied strictly in a situation where employment in large scale units is growing more slowly than the labourforce, would tend to discrimate in skill training against groups currently under represented in large scale employing units.

In other words, people who might have gained entrance to skills training in a situation where educational qualifications were the sole criterion, would now face an explicit or implicit additional hurdle of employer acceptability. Also, a move towards a more in-service than pre-service training system would tend to favour those already employed. As Table 4.15 clearly indicates such a situation would still be very disadvantageous to women despite some gains in representation in the 1980s.

One consequence of such a situation is that self-employment schemes will find themselves catering for those actually less technically (and often socially in terms of age and gender) qualified to set-up a viable, profitable business than people employed in large scale units. To be successful in enabling employment and human resource development in both large scale and small scale units, the government needs to ensure movements of higher skilled people into the small scale sector and lower skilled people into the large scale sector.

TABLE 4.15

Female Representation by Occupation (Percentage of Workers in Occupations who are Female) Based on 1973 HED Survey and 1981 Census

	Professional and related workers	Administrative and managerial workers	Clerical and related workers
1973 (HED Data)	9.0	4.0	2.0
1981 (Population Census)	15.0	2.0	3.0
Labour Force Survey			
1984-85	15.5	2.3	1.7
1985-86	17.3	1.8	1.5
1986-87	17.4	4.3	2.7
1987-88	18.3	2.7	2.9

Source 1973 HED Survey, *1981 PopulationCensus*, in Kazi 1990.

To achieve these goals requires a mixture of positive encouragement and positive discrimination respectively. Positive encouragement to mature, skilled workers to set up their own enterprises can be provided by targeting small scale industry promotion packages on this group as much as young people or poor women.

Positive discrimination can operate through identifying skills in critical shortage and channelling people from under-represented groups onto training courses for those skills (in the case of women this could be relatively easily achieved by providing gender specific facilities). In these actions, the government would be enabling both skilled and unskilled people to pursue wider options and, to that aim would be willing to work against the immediate interest of the controllers of large scale employing units.

CHAPTER 5

Opportunities and Constraints with Respect to Productive Employment Creation Outside the Large Scale Employing Sector

5.1 Choice at the Household Level

The interplay of fast growing labour supply and slower growing formal sector labour demand expresses itself at the household level as choices and constraints over size of household, education, control of land and other assets, skill acquisition, migration, mechanisation, casualisation and access to regular employment in the large scale employing sector. This situation of constrained choice can also flow over into political and cultural areas of life.

The data provided by Labour Force Surveys do yield information on employment, industrial and occupational composition and breakdown by age, sex and educational level. Although fairly detailed classification can be had, the data are inadequate in linking labour force participation to various types of households differentiated on the basis of their asset holdings, income level, or the occupation of the head of the household. Very few studies did try to understand the nexus between households' positions in society and the work pattern of their members.

One of the major limitations of most state planned development strategies in the past has been the non-incorporation of the household decision-making process in the design of the policies. There is a need to recognise the fact that most, if not all, decisions taken at the household level are interdependent and integrated. Policy may aim to work through isolated compartments but households may respond by diverting resources or manipulating regulations as an aspect of achieving an optimum position for the household, not for society.

Inter-relationships between, for instance, household productive and reproductive patterns, economic activity time allocation between individuals in the household, and locational decisions regarding the various members of the household are based on circumstances and experience which are an integrated, dynamic whole for the household decision-making process.

Policy intervention must take into account household objectives and the ultimate impact on the welfare of the society. There is a need to devise such policies which facilitate a synchronisation between individual and social gains. Of special concern are the calculations which determine reproductive, education, and economic activity behaviour at the household level.

An additional child may be seen as a strength for family welfare but, when cumulated with many similar decisions by other households, as a cost for society. Socio-economic factors operating at the household level influence its reproductive decisions. These may explain the continuing, high fertility rates in Pakistan. Conventional approaches stress improving female education and health statuses, which are measured as low in Pakistan by international standards (World Bank 1989). But even if education and health were improved, the opportunity cost to a household of child-caring time and energy might still be low given women's predominant economic activity is low productivity, low income self/household employment.

Households' assessments regarding benefits and costs of children are based on a variety of factors. The flow of expected income and its variation over time, the nature of demand for child labour in the household organisation of production, and opportunity costs of time and material inputs in raising and educating the children exert their influence on decision-making by households on whether to take active measures to limit fertility.

Wide differentials exist between households in the labour force participation of children belonging to the age group of 10-14 years. The factors underlying these varying patterns have importance also for schooling as human resource development.

The education system of Pakistan has undergone a considerable quantitative expansion over time. But the literacy rate (usually identified with completed primary education in Pakistan) is at present around 30 per cent (46 per cent for urban areas and 22 per cent for rural areas). The literacy rate for males (41 per cent) is substantially higher than the females (17.7 per cent), with females in the rural areas showing a nine per cent literacy rate for 1986-87. The education system also suffers from a high rate of drop out at primary and secondary levels. For instance, cumulative drop outs during 1976 to 1985 were 47 per cent for males and 62 per cent for females for the primary classes. In the case of secondary education, these rates were 53 per cent and 47 per cent respectively. The drop out rates are much higher for rural areas than for urban areas.

There are still limitations on the supply side of the schooling system (social expenditure on education is around 2.6 per cent of the GNP which hardly compares favourably with 3.4 per cent of the GNP by the public sector alone for the lower middle income countries as a whole, but there is a need to identify the factors operating on the demand side of the education.

The rational behaviour of the parents and the household in investing in the children may be partly responsible for explaining the high drop out rates and low enrollment rates. Child work may reflect an effort on the part of parents as a more useful form of education to ensure their children are trained in a particular vocation or skill. Children working in workshops could be seen as acquiring training in the "Ustad-Shagird" system. Children may be physically needed to participate in household production at peak labour times of the year or even for the whole year. Much child work in the rural areas may fall under this heading. Only after accounting for the above, can working children be considered as economically active due to household poverty alone.

It has been observed that labour force participation by children is higher and adult women lower among the middle size land owning classes. In urban areas one finds also a high correlation between the self-employment of father and child work. The occupational status of the head of the household may be a major determinant in this context (Irfan 1989).

Generally, the nature of job in terms of occupation and industry as well as employment status appears to be determined for secondary earners, defined as non-heads of household, by what the head of the household is doing or the asset position of the household. The data contained in PLM Survey 1979 indicates that there is very high correlation between the occupation of the head of the household and non-head household male member. The same is true for industry and employment status. An observation consistent with the fact that 70 per cent of the labour force is self employed in a predominantly household enterprise system.

The existence of choice in household behaviour is indicated by comparisons between incomes of the self-employed and those of wage earners which do not identify the self-employed as the most poverty stricken or least paid group. In addition, studies of production functions in rural areas of Pakistan are suggestive of the fact that marginal products of children and women are greater than zero. Thus, patterns of labour utilisation within the household economy cannot be regarded as lacking choice or economically irrational and, thus, easily alterable by policy.

In terms of policy impact, it can be argued that poor households in the rural areas, for instance, rationally choose not to participate in the facilities extended by the state because of the cost as well as the perception that the labour market decisions are not class neutral. In other words, they do not believe that through getting their children, especially daughters, educated, they would experience either an inter-generation upward mobility or higher level of status and income. The correlation between enrollment ratio of the children and some of the characteristics of the household and rates of return to primary education does suggest that the significant private benefits assumed in education policy are not justified, and merely increasing the supply of places may be insufficient to radically raise school attendance.

But on the other hand, for middle income households present policy pronouncements and activities may be giving signals to households about good employment prospects for those with academic qualifications in the 1990s, especially in the public sector. Following such signals, it is rational under current uncertainties, for households to choose to "position" members in terms of education/location/contact networks to contest more effectively for scarce, but highly desirable large scale sector employment opportunities at the cost of planning for other possibilities.

Policies aimed at reducing fertility or raising school attendance in the social interest must be sensitive to the rationality of household choices. Policies need to be targeted and sensitive towards the real circumstances faced by households with very differing characteristics. The need for state planning is to create a structure for identifying and enabling specific plans for productive employment generation at the household level drawing on all the various resources which the household possesses, and complementing them appropriately.

5.2 The Migration Choice

Household income, demographic behaviour and decisions regarding participation in the labour market are intimately related with the choice of location for household members. Data collected by censuses and surveys can provide information regarding direction and level of flow on the basis of region or districts. Estimates can be made of gross or net out-migration and in-migration at the district level. The data sources in general provide little insight into the factors operating at the household level which have influenced the pattern of mobility of its members.

Rural to rural migration has received little attention at the hands of the researchers. One of the reasons presumably being the belief that a substantial portion of the rural migration may be reflective of women moving on marriage, though this may have significance in terms of understanding relationships between households and intra-rural resource shifts.

Most research studies based on specialised surveys have been confined to rural-urban migration. The flow of remittances back to rural households can constitute a substantial portion of the total income of the household and feedback into household economic activity decisions in the rural areas. The incidence of migration from the rural areas to urban areas appears to be the highest among the most educated males (Irfan et al. 1983).

Labour migration to the Gulf region has been very important for remittance receiving households. As sending a family member abroad involves a substantial cost which may have been beyond the capacity of the majority of the lower income households, participation of the poorest households has been proportionately lower compared to that of middle income households. There is also a positive association between family size and the percentage of potential labour force members (10 years and above) outside the household, within Pakistan or abroad.

Migration patterns indicate that the migration of a member of a household is frequently not a concern of that individual alone and patterns of resource availability may be changed in both the destination and source areas, yielding opportunities and constraints with respect to new economic activity. The National Manpower Commission to some extent recognises this situation in its discussion and recommendations on encouraging returning international labour migrants to use their savings and skills more productively. But the Commission does not give any explanation of the conflicting pressures on the return migrants with respect to household consumption and status demands.

5.3 Women's Lack of Choice

To say that households have choices is not the same as saying that all individuals within households have choices. Women's constraints certainly appear to be much greater than their choices in Pakistan. A simple typology will be used in this section to bring out the range of specific constraints that women face with respect to gaining access to productive economic activity. The four categories used in the following typology will not be equally relevant to the experiences of all women. However, these categories are four different aspects of the more fundamental experience of gender discrimination that all women share in Pakistan. Many women will be experiencing a mix of problems associated with all categories; problems which are largely of men's choosing or making.

(a) Poor socio-psychological conditions, especially with respect to career development:

Informal discussions with women administrators indicate strong feelings that career development procedures (including transfers, in-service training and promotions) are not founded on clear, explicit meritocratic principles, which leaves room for arbitrary decisions where gender prejudices can operate. Such women think that the general necessity for recognition of personnel on the basis of their merit and competence would be especially to their benefit.

Gender distinctions also emerged in training differentials between men and women factory workers reported in Hafeez (1989). According to managers interviewed, although women were not necessarily totally excluded from areas of training, more men than women have received training in machine operation, laboratory work, weaving and spinning. No managers from any Province stated that technical training or apprenticeship were provided to women in their factories.

In the same nationwide survey of women factory workers reported in Hafeez (1989), nearly 70 per cent of managers said that women workers had lesser opportunities for promotion than the men. Many more women aspired to a better job within a factory in which they worked than those who expressed confidence that they would actually achieve this goal. Few managers actually gave explicit reasons for the promotion of a higher proportion of male compared to female workers.

Women are under pressure to stay in locations where they have lived for some time. Generally speaking, it is much more acceptable for women to reside in a hostel while they are studying than while they are working. A woman in Pakistan is expected to live only with her husband and children which leads to hostel facilities in certain small towns being underutilised. Another reason for a reluctance to take promotions away from present location and family is perhaps a deeper fear that they might be molested or otherwise harmed, even though this may appear as stated dissatisfaction with housing facilities or transportation services. In areas of exceptional socio-political tension, married women like to work not only in the city or town they inhabit but also prefer to work near their houses.

The psychological consequences of these socially imposed restrictions on career development need to be recognised and programmes of career development instituted that deal explicitly with the specific problems of talented women facing psychological pressures not to fully express those talents as a result of men's prejudices at work and in wider society.

(b) Poor physical conditions at work:

Few women workers in factories in the Hafeez (1989) study stated that they had access to supportive facilities and services at work to relieve the burdens imposed by men- oriented society. 80 per cent of the women interviewed did not have access to child care, 61 per cent to transport, 71 per cent to transport allowance, 89 per cent to an accommodation or house allowance, 71 per cent to medical facility, 63 per cent to social security, 76 per cent to latrines, 59 per cent to wash rooms, 60 per cent to allowance for children, and 86 per cent to any training facility.

But many women did not dislike their jobs despite the poor working environment. Only 19 per cent expressed stress because of their working environment. As revealed in Hafeez (1989), employers' rationales for hiring women are embedded in perceived personality traits of women workers such as docility or obedience which contribute to stability in the workplace and which facilitate low cost production and little need to adjust management policies to workers' demands. In the study, male managers did not indicate the "purdah" norm as the reason for not hiring men in departments where women worked. The reasons attributed by them in response to an open ended question for preferring women to work in segregated departments related to the "easy" nature of work and perceived feminine attributes of women workers such as docility (see also Khan 1988). Poor working conditions are unlikely to be challenged by such workers themselves without state support.

(c) Poor economic conditions with respect to low pay and insecurity for contract workers and legally unrecognised women workers, especially home workers:

Under conditions of growing unemployment and underemployment, there is a tendency for employers to exploit opportunities for reducing the economic rewards of employees. Under different circumstances, this may involve casualisation of directly employed labour, obtaining labour through unscrupulous labourcontractors, and debt-bonding of men to provide not only their own labour but women household members also.

Such practices remove men and women even further from legislative protection available to "regulated" sector workers and ensure that men's rates of earnings are set at a bare, physiological subsistence level for a small household, and women's rates of earnings are below men's.

In addition, an unmeasured number of women work isolated in their homes depriving them of any possibility and therefore benefits of collective bargaining. There are probably at least two million such women, usually working out of economic necessity and accepting unconditionally the terms of work laid down by the contractor. Many women home-workers are reported to receive less than Rs. 5.00 per day for a full day's economic activity, which would be insufficient to purchase food and fuel to feed adequately one adult in 1990 (Mohiuddin 1987). Given the isolated conditions under which these women work they effectively fall outside the realm of all protective labour laws.

(d) *Poor cultural conditions with respect to restriction and discrimination in access to education and jobs:*

At a national conference on "Women in Mainstream Development" in Islamabad in 1990, an eminent Pakistani woman expressed the view that women in Pakistan are culturally socialised to believe that "the career world is an alien territory". No matter what they contribute women will remain cultural immigrants in such a world. And as immigrants, they are channelled by the dominant culture into low status and low productivity work on the most spurious of quasi-genetic grounds.

Compared to men, women are likely to never enter schooling, or to be withdrawn at an early age. As adults, women are also more influenced by their parents and spouses in choosing lines of employment and quitting employment altogether. Strategies that some women with schooling may use to escape partially from such attitudes about barriers to their employment are not marrying, marrying later, and making non-arranged marriages, though this also can have heavy cultural costs.

Generally, a family-selected, culturally-protected environment is a major criterion for choosing a specific line and place of work. In the Hafeez (1989) study, 31 per cent of women factory workers stated that relatives and 19 per cent that their husbands worked in the factories where they themselves worked.

In addition to these pressures, women are culturally expected to take and generally do take responsibility for domestic activity, which is vital to the reproduction of a healthy society as economic activity is vital to the production of a sustainable economy. The time and energy required for domestic activity needs to be explicitly taken into account in designing and appraising programmes and projects centred on economic activity.

For programmes and projects which assume availability of women's time and energy, it is important that nothing be assumed about availability. For such programmes and projects, the casual appearance of women's economic inactivity can be seen as neither the same as the reality of women's economic inactivity (especially within the home) nor the same as women having time or energy to spare from a double burden of economic and domestic activity (Khan and Bilquees 1976). Time-budget analysis, as recommended in Chapter 3, has a role to play in showing the reality of women's lives. But such analysis does not directly reveal energy availability, especially reductions in energy availability through illness. Morbidity (as well as income) analysis is always a useful complement to time-budget analysis.

Increasing choices for women will be a major theme in the final chapter.

5.4 Patterns of Household Negatives to Growing Labour Market Imbalances

Faced with a growing labour market imbalance in the 1990s, falling especially heavily on the young with primary education in the first half of the decade, there are a number of ways in which households and their individual members can react with varying aggregate social consequences.

(a) Where households have access to secure, higher incomes and/or means of livelihood, it may be possible for individuals to withdraw from the labour force and reduce education costs and share existing activities between more members of the household. This response may be viewed as a desirable response in terms of social costs, and likely given the experience of non-participation of women in outside employment and that children in formal education is widespread and culturally acceptable. However, the number of households which can afford withdrawal is falling and the withdrawal of women and the need to maximise opportunities of finding outside income in an active child labour market will be no disincentive to controlling fertility with high, longer run social costs.

(b) Individuals and households may relocate to areas of higher probabilities of obtaining employment, even if these probabilities and associated expected incomes are still low. With many households now having experience of relatively successful migration, internal migration in Pakistan (in the absence of international migration opportunities) could be a common choice involving high social costs in terms of infrastructure demands and social tension.

(c) The growing strains within households of prolonged job searches, and disappointed expectations will produce tendencies for households to split along lines where potential for survival or improvement in quality of life of one part is significantly increased at the cost of the remaining part. The "remaining" household constituted by the second part will be more vulnerable to poverty due to age (old or young) and/or gender mix. This process will involve some deliberate decisions but could be a matter of drift as migrant members reduce contact, or irretrievable emotional breakdown accompanied by violence. The access of the new household heads to income earning opportunities will be very limited and there will be a growing presence of, increasingly visible, households in absolute poverty with low economic activity potential, especially female-headed households.

(d) Illegal activity is a matter of opportunity and motivation. In the 1980s, Pakistan has seen a growth in the opportunity to traffic in narcotics. There has also been a growth in private ownership of weapons to protect that traffic and engage in other illegal activity for economic gain, notably kidnapping (see Table 5.1). Lack of access to legal employment opportunities is not a necessary condition, nor does it justify illegal activity, but it does not diminish the motivation to engage in such activities. Economic need and psychological/cultural alienation will grow in the 1990s as contributors to such motivation. Law and order policy will need to be consistently firm in the 1990s, alongside any proposed enabling employment strategy, if legal employment is not to appear a poor option by comparison for a small, but crucially significant, portion of young male society.

(e) Political demands for targeted special employment treatment on ethnic, spatial, poverty, education grounds will continue to multiply. The experience of young people entering the labour market in the 1990s will be compared unfavourably with the experience of parents and elder siblings and interpretations at individual, household and group levels that political discrimination is the cause and potentially the solution to their particular problem of obtaining employment will be easily drawn. Precedents for political preferment in access to public sector employment are now firmly set. Frustration will appear in aggregate as political volatility.

TABLE 5.1

Serious Crime Statistics, 1971-89

Crimes	1971	1975	1980	1985	1986	1987	1988	1989*
Murder	3982	4625	4548	5453	6075	6404	6807	3744
Dacoity	130	99	85	248	340	307	366	273
Robbery	1104	497	518	910	1255	1186	1318	788
Burglary	13232	10285	8579	8914	8499	8190	8525	4500
Riots	1868	1591	1941	2291	2593	2475	2374	1505
Abduction/ Kidnapping	3065	3022	4599	5064	5155	5124	5089	2868
Rape	636	567	1025	1512	1602	1624	1715	895
Child lifting	33	46	66	85	102	130	94	61
Cattle Theft	8541	9232	4755	4597	5598	3783	4721	3026
Other Theft	20091	19134	24732	16404	19915	19202	22871	6333
Others	76997	115321	113738	174557	180591	199021	213811	125861

*Upto June.

Source: Bureau of Police Research and Development, Ministry of Interior in *Economic Survey 1988-89* Statistical Supplement, Finance Division, Government of Pakistan, 1989.

The above decisions made at the household level to cope with the growing labour market imbalance will, in aggregate, involve social costs and tend to shift the pressure of adjustment onto women and younger men. The pressure on women will feed through to children and the elderly and present itself as a poverty problem. The pressure on young men will present itself as a law and order problem. Such individual/household rational responses will, in aggregate, impose heavy economic and social costs on Pakistan. Impoverisation, urbanisation, and criminalisation are processes which produce strong popular demands for government action and diversion of resources from private sector productive investment and public sector positive development activities. State policy in the 1990s will need to be as even-handed and firm in disabling socially costly activities as in enabling socially productive activities.

Alongside socially costly responses, there exists socially productive planning to generate productive employment on the basis of all the human resources and other resource potentials available to the household. The challenge of enabling people to bring such plans to fruition, fairly distinguish and prioritise claims, spread costs and benefits, and curtail competing anti-social activities is the challenge for Pakistan state planners in the 1990s.

5.5 The Development Potential of Small Scale Employing Units

Every middle income household with its mixture of human and other resources is a potential small scale employing unit offering economic activity to two members of the household and two or three wage employees.

The discussion of small scale employing units frequently becomes bogged down in attempts to arrive at a precise definition of this "informal" sector. Often, this sector is delineated by using negative definitions such as the unregistered sector or the one which does not abide by labour laws. At times, the connotation of the term may be stretched to include socially undesirable activities such as the "black market/money" economy or the group of people who do not pay taxes.

But, the informal sector may well provide job opportunities as well as subsistence income to the majority of the population. Estimation of the actual size of the informal sector is made in Pakistan by treating it as a residual sector (total employment minus formal employment). This procedure was used by Guisinger and Irfan (1980) and in a recent study conducted by the World Bank (1988). These studies indicate that over three-fifths of total employment is believed to be in the informal sector.

Studies also lend the impression that a disaggregated picture of the informal sector represents a wide spectrum on the income distribution scale. Whilst a significant proportion of households may be earning on the average less than their counterparts in the formal sector, there are people engaged in the informal sector who earned much more than those with the same human and physical assets in the formal sector.

In a multi-variate regression analysis, Guisinger and Irfan found that the differential in earnings due to formal and informal location of employment is not substantial. In order to enable the informal sector to be in a position to generate productive job opportunities, both the constraints to its growth as well as the sources of its growth must be reckoned in any policy relevant exercise. The type of facilities needed by those who are engaged in the informal sector must be identified and actual delivery mechanism needs to be understood. For instance, availability of credit can be cited as an example where the lending institutions require collateral and formal application procedures. The extent to which these restrictions discourage households from getting credit or even applying for credit need to be understood. Procedures should be adopted wherein credit is made more easily available in practice as well as in theory.

In order to generate sufficient employment to absorb the growing labour force in productive activities, it is now generally accepted that state planners should allocate resources towards small scale manufacturing industries, especially in rural areas to discourage socially costly rural-urban migration. This acceptance rests on the belief that small scale industries require far less capital to generate one employment opportunity than is required in the large scale manufacturing sector. While the Systems (Pvt.) Ltd. report (1990) raises empirical doubts on the underestimation of large scale manufacturing employment, nevertheless the argument that small scale manufacturing has a strong employment potential still holds.

In order to understand the dynamics of small scale manufacturing industry, two independent surveys of small scale manufacturing industry, one rural (Aftab 1990) and one urban (Nadvi,1990) are discussed here. Sampling design for surveys of small scale units is difficult due to lack of information on the population of such units, therefore both surveys sought to cover a range of locations and sectors rather than seek formal statistical representativeness.

The rural survey interviewed in 600 units in all four provinces while the urban survey covered 328 units in two cities. The surveys were both undertaken by the Federal Bureau of Statistics in 1989.

The structure of small scale industry was previously investigated in a Federal Bureau of Statistics survey in 1983/4 (see Table 5.2 A). The Bureau has subsequently undertaken a census operation in 1987 but this is not yet published. Table 5.2 and Table 3 in Annex I to this Report from the Project rural industry survey indicate a diversity of activities whose only common aspect is being small-scale in terms of employing around five workers (see Tables 1 and 2 of Annex I) or having total fixed asets of less than Rs. 30,00,000 in 1983/4 (Table 5.2 B).

TABLE 5.2(A)

Composition of Rural And Urban Small Scale Industries, 1983/84

(Per cent)

	No. of Firms		Value of F. Assets		No. of Workers	
	Rural	Urban	Rural	Urban	Rural	Urban
Food, beverage & tobacco	44.2	18.2	63.3	39.6	48.6	18.5
Textile and leather	12.7	30.0	4.6	20.0	11.1	33.4
Wood & wood products	15.2	14.5	13.6	11.0	13.9	13.7
Chemicals, rubber, plastics	0.6	1.7	1.0	1.5	0.8	2.0
Non-metallic minerals	5.5	3.0	9.0	1.7	10.4	1.9
Fabricated metals	17.3	16.4	3.7	16.6	12.6	17.2
Other	4.2	16.2	1.2	9.6	2.6	13.3

Note: Only establishments with total fixed assets of Rs 3 million or less are included.
Source: SSHMI, 1983/84 in World Bank, 1989.

This diversity is not only between sectors and between rural and urban but within sectors in the rural areas as indicated by the differences between the asset structures of units in rainfed as compared to irrigated areas. Generalisations are difficult to make but it would appear that units in rainfed areas are less diverse, older, and larger in fixed assets than units in irrigated areas. If this observation is accurate, it might suggest a policy towards rainfed area industrialisation emphasising creation of units and a policy in irrigated areas emphasising growth of existing units. The urban survey also showed large standard deviations in the distribution of owner-estimated current values of plant and machinery within sectors, indicating the desirability of treating units as individuals. The diversity of existing small scale manufacturing between and within locations and sectors in Pakistan is heartening but demands policy flexibility. State planning should lay down broad principles and leave application to local officials accountable primarily to their clients.

In terms of problems in starting a small scale unit, the urban survey results in Table 1 of Annex II show capital/credit most frequently mentioned (38.9 per cent) followed by problems in obtaining raw materials (16.9 per cent) and identifying a

TABLE 5.2 (B)

Comparison of Rural and Small Manufacturing Establishments 1983/84

	Average Employment per establishment (# workers)		Fixed Assets per Establishment (Rs. '000)		Fixed Assets per Worker (Rs.'000)		Value Added/ Worker (Rs. '000)		Receipts from Others % of Value Added	
	Rural	Urban	Rural	Urban	Rural	Urban	Rural	Urban	Rural	Urban
Food, beverage, tobacco	2.5	2.3	24.1	46.1	9.7	13.2	7.3	24.0	45.6	18.5
Textile & leather	2.0	2.6	6.1	14.2	3.1	7.0	8.6	12.9	38.9	45.7
Wood & wood products	2.1	2.2	15.3	16.1	7.3	7.4	9.6	10.8	78.3	53.2
Chemicals, rubber, plastics	3.4	2.6	31 9	19.1	9.5	7.3	29.0	16.3	1.6	26.5
Non-Metallic minerals	4.3	2.0	27.9	11.8	6.4	6.9	32.8	34.4	0.7	2.1
Fabricated Metals	1.6	2.4	7.1	21.5	4.3	10.2	7.7	12.2	76.5	41.6
Others [1]	1.4	1.8	4.9	12.8	7.4	7.0	10.4	15.1	82.3	62.5
All Establishments	2.3	2.3	17.0	21.3	7.4	9.2	10.8	15.5	54.1	38.3

[1] Includes paper and paper products, basic metals.

Source SSMMI 1983/84 in World Bank, 1989.

market (12.5 per cent). Lack of technical skills accounted for 7.9 per cent of responses. Factors other than credit as candidates for inclusion in an assistance package appear to be specific not only to sector and location but also to individual units, indicating the desirability of flexibility in the package offered.

Credit also frequently appears as a current problem in both the rural and urban surveys. Table 5 of Annex I shows around 70 per cent of rural units claiming to be constrained by lack of capital followed by about 40 per cent mentions of market constraints. Specific skills and technology constraints were rarely mentioned. Similarly, the urban survey (see Table 3 of Annex II) found 51 per cent named capital/credit and 23 per cent named market and competition problems. Again employment and human resource development questions did not feature significantly. The policy packages outlined in the concluding chapter for starting and expanding small scale units accept they must be credit-led and include the possibility of working capital as well as fixed capital advances. Most rural units not only desired credit but in general terms claimed they could afford to repay loans, suggesting that access in terms of collateral and/or procedures rather than credit terms is a major obstacle.

A uniformity between rural and urban units can also be seen in the estimates of growth performance over the last three years when the overall Pakistan economy has grown about twenty per cent. Table 4 of Annex I shows only 29 out of 600 rural small scale units declared growth of more than ten per cent in the last three years. Table 2 of Annex II shows 72 per cent of the 179 urban units to whom the question was relevant declaring that in the past three years output had not changed or had slightly decreased. There are methodological and interpretation problems in using one-shot questionnaire data on existing small scale units to assess past growth patterns but these responses do suggest a sector which is dynamic in terms of increasing numbers of units, but not in terms of increasing activity within units.

On the basis of this tentative data, it may well be the case that small scale units are growing in net numbers (with a significant attrition rate) but not expanding once a low level equilibrium in credit/market/technology/employment is achieved. If this is the case then the policy question is less about establishing small scale units but more about their survival and subsequent growth from employing three or four workers to six or eight.

There appear to be great obstacles to such growth, which an economist would see as a high marginal cost of expansion. Obtaining credit, supervising additional labour, scrapping existing machinery and purchasing new machinery, finding additional demand appear to combine to produce this high marginal cost. The image of small scale units using the household's funds to employ local labour with limited skills at a subsistence wage with second-hand tools/machinery to serve a few local customers is, by and large, confirmed by the surveys. To double the size of such units and raise labour productivity accordingly is more of a challenge to policy than to assist the creation of micro-units which would probably have occurred autonomously, at least in urban and irrigated areas.

Neither rural or urban units show significant contact with the state. In the rural survey, 29 units out of the 600 reported contact with assisting agencies and 12 reported being registered with regulatory agencies; in the urban survey, five units out of 328 reported credit from state agencies while over 50 reported paying bribes to state officials. Much could be done in terms of the quantity and quality of contact.

The workers in rural units are predominantly male (see Tables 1 and 2 in Annex 1) and only two women wage workers were found in the 328 units in the urban survey (though 6.5 per cent of urban units were owned by women). How far this low representation of women is accurate and how far it is a sampling and methodological product is an open question, as in neither survey was the use of women's labour positively probed as a specific issue.

Rural unit workers were reported to be predominantly local, with the only significant exception being the brick kiln sector which is notorious for its mobile bonded labour system. Half the 592 urban wage workers interviewed claimed to have obtained their job on a relatively open market basis, and 79 per cent reported a job search period of less than a month. 49 per cent of urban wage workers also said they had received training in a previous job also indicating some market choice for urban workers in changing employment after training.

Few rural and urban units reported any significant seasonality/lay-off periods, and certainly the urban wage workers appear to have full-time regular work and be paid the same rate as the contract workers in large scale units at just over Rs. 1,000 a month. Gauging the full-time equivalent monthly pay of rural wage workers is difficult from the survey, but the 1:2 differentials measured in the 1983/4 survey (see Table 5.3) may well still exist, despite the faster increases in rural wages from their lower base.

TABLE 5.3

Urban and Rural Wages in Small-Scale Manufacturing, 1983/84

	Urban	Rural
Employment Cost/Worker (Rs '000) [1]	2.34	1.31
Food, Beverages, Tobacco	2.71	0.85
Textiles and Leather	3.00	1.74
Wood & Wood Products	2.03	1.45
Chemicals, Rubber, Plastic	2.59	3.20
Non-Metallic Minerals	1.77	3.82
Fabricated Metals	0.36	0.52
Other	0.89	0.42
Growth in Real Wages, 1977-1984 (%) [2]	23.0	40.7

1 Employment cost consists largely (over 95%) of wages Figures include both household and manufacturing units.

2 For urban, data sources are SSHMI, 1976/77, 1983/84; for rural, data are from Irfan and Ahmad, 1984

Source. SSHMI 1983/84 in World Bank, 1989.

But a pressure towards equilibrating labour market conditions is shown clearly in Tables 4 and 5 of Annex II, 35 per cent of urban small scale unit wage workers, who migrated to their present urban location, came in the expectation of higher income, and 62 per cent of all urban small scale unit wage workers interviewed would prefer to be working in a large scale unit in the private or public sector (as would 30 per cent of owners). Only 13 per cent would prefer to set up a unit of their own. Raising productivity and incomes in rural and urban small scale units is necessary to reduce labour supply pressures on the urban, large scale sector.

But skill training as a route to such increased productivity will meet resistance in urban areas and have logistical problems in rural areas. Urban owners do not see skill training as a constraint. The majority of owners claim to have primary education or less (70 per cent) and few have had any formal training. 80 per cent of urban owners claim no problem in finding skilled workers and the owners, preference would be for on-site training with 90 per cent expressing no willingness to share training costs.

In some contrast, while 70 per cent of rural owners also have primary education or less, 50 per cent of owners of rural units express an interest in relatively formal courses (though no financial implications were mentioned), which would be difficult to organise for dispersed units in a variety of sectors. The strategic approach of focusing training on the needs of larger scale units does receive support from these observations.

But if large scale units are going to act as centres of skill diffusion and breeding grounds for new household initiated small scale units, then complementary linkages between large and small scale units are needed. The urban survey does show evidence of a variety of such linkages, though it is difficult to distinguish between ones where the larger unit is predominantly complementing the smaller and those where the larger is predominantly exploiting the smaller. Only 5 out of 600 rural small scale units reported sub-contracting links with large scale units. State planners can enable the exploration of complementarities and see how production processes can be broken down into labour intensive and capital intensive activities.

The argument that identically consumer attractive products can be produced by less labour intensive technology in the small scale manufacturing sector than in the large scale manufacturing sector, increasingly including the international sector in Pakistan, has not been convincingly documented by its proponents. It follows that instead of arguing just for small scale activities it would be far better to argue for such large scale manufacturing industries which could have substantial subcontracting possibilities for small scale producers.

In this regard, engineering industries can be further promoted which all over the world have been developed on the basis of large scale producers and many subcontractors. In Pakistan, tractor manufacturing provides an excellent example of such a relationship. Large scale investment should be profitable in those industries which have a large potential in labour-intensive downstream units which can be established in the small scale manufacturing sector, given Pakistan's relatively low labour costs.

Industries which have strong backward and forward linkages especially with the small scale sector could be promoted to generate more employment rather than seeking for a reallocation of resources from large scale producers to the small scale producers.

This strategic approach does differ from the consumer led market infrastructure recommendations of the National Manpower Commission but is in line with the Commission's thinking on technical and locational support infrastructure. It is to this approach of seeking complementarities between larger and smaller employing units that we shall return at greater length in the final chapter.

CHAPTER 6

The Policy Framework for Enabling Productive Employment Generation in Pakistan in the 1990s

6.1 Background to an Enabling Strategy Formulation

The labour force in Pakistan is currently growing at more than three per cent per annum. Population growth in the 1970s and 1980s at about the same rate means that the labour force will almost certainly continue to grow at this rate through the 1990s and into the first decade of the twenty-first century. Even if significant overseas labour emigration opportunities re-emerge, this will only have a limited effect on the productive employment challenge in Pakistan given the large absolute numbers of people involved.

In addition to this simple extrapolation from current trends, there are two other factors to be considered on the labour supply side. The labour force participation rate of women is low by international standards, and it is probable that more women will wish to join the labour force as economic pressures increase on many households. Also success in increasing the demand for labour may itself induce some additional increases in numbers of people declaring themselves available for economic activity. These factors increasing the labour supply are likely to be larger than increased enrollment in secondary schooling and frustrated withdrawal in decreasing the labour supply.

The demand for labour in large-scale manufacturing and agricultural sectors in the 1990s is unlikely to increase at a rate sufficient to absorb even the basic extrapolated labour force growth rate. Both sectors are showing tendencies to stress improving quality, exportability and profitability through investment in machinery rather than through employing more workers. Given current low levels of labour productivity, this stress is not altogether undesirable and should not be totally discouraged, but it does mean that growth in the total value added in these sectors will continue to generate half or less that growth rate in employment.

If macroeconomic GNP growth targets of around 6.5 per cent per annum are achieved during the Seventh Plan period and maintained for the rest of the decade then, with positive policies towards preventing a fall in the overall elasticity of employment with respect to increasing value-added, it will be possible to utilise around 2.6 per cent per annum of the likely 3.5 per cent per annum increase in the labour force in the relatively formal activities as they are conventionally measured in Pakistan.

In addition to this formal sector employment generation, autonomous self- and small-scale employment generation will make a vital contribution to bringing the labour market towards balance. The contribution of small-scale industry to this is difficult to quantify, but limitations on the supply side and demand side in producing consumer acceptable output at competitive prices should temper optimism about such activity automatically absorbing the remaining future increase in the labour force, let alone making inroads into the existing deficit in availability of satisfying, adequately rewarding employment. Many, possibly a majority, of small-scale manufacturing enterprises will fail to economically survive and the winding up of such enterprises will itself produce social and financial disruption for the entrepreneur, worker, and input supplier households closely associated with the enterprise. Coping with bankruptcies needs to be built into assistance policies.

Any market with a structural imbalance will show two types of responses. Firstly, a direct price response which will tend to ration scarcity and discourage abundance. Secondly, a rent response in which those who have power in the market (often aptly labelled as gate-keepers) attempt to make gains at the expense of those who do not have power by charging for access.

But the labour market is not just another market. Through the labour market, people gain the ability to survive and better their lives and in economic activity they gain a considerable amount of their sense of social, and individual, value.

With a growing deficit of satisfying, adequately rewarding employment and a resulting tendency for rates of earnings to fall and power over the labour market to become more concentrated, any employment strategy would be irresponsible if it did not take likely household level economic, demographic, cultural, and political negative responses from below seriously. Policy must recognise that such responses are often rational for the individual or household and will not be halted by mere exhortation or passing legislation. Positive alternatives for socially positive economic activity must be offered.

There are households, especially in rural areas, where an element of autonomy from the open labour market exists. Control over land or some other productive assets may allow work-sharing and consumption-sharing within the household without undue strain. But population growth is making such situations rarer.

More affluent households may be willing to tolerate consumption-sharing but it is unlikely to be indefinitely acceptable and resources will be put into paying rents to gain privileged access to employment opportunities to the resentment of the wider society.

For many households, the problem will appear as a prolonged employment search by individual members involving strain on resources and relationships.

Initial unrealistic expectations of a relatively undemanding office position in the public sector will be lowered eventually but not without considerable resentment.

While the general trend towards de-regulation will reduce opportunities for economic rents in other markets, the labour market will be vulnerable to increased manipulation by informal job-brokers in the private and public sectors. Vulnerabilities and networks will be exploited and the parallel labour market will tend to grow with merit being only one criterion, and possibly a declining criterion.

Market forces can only successfully allocate resources where an equilibrium between demand and supply exists at a price which is socio-politically acceptable or at least enforceable. The market-clearing price for labour in Pakistan will increasingly lie outside that range in the 1990s. Similarly, regulation can only be successful when the personal rewards from evasion are small relative to the likely punishment. In Pakistan, this is not the case at this time. Therefore, an active parallel labour market will be a feature of the Pakistan economy in the 1990s. The aim of policy in this area should be to make merit an active consideration in that market and check abuses of power.

Thus, without positive new initiatives in the private sector facilitated by the public sector, present trends suggest a fast increasing labour supply by historical and international comparative standards and much slower increase in labour demand in key sectors. This growing imbalance will have negative economic, cultural, and political effects.

State planning must aim at creating an environment which will enable people to implement their own plans for provision of more, more productive employment. State planning and coordination is needed to ensure coverage of all promising locations and lines of activity; the offer of appropriate multi-element support for all feasible initiatives from individuals in all socio-economic groups; and an equitable sharing of costs within the private sector and between the private and public sectors with no "free-riding" by affluent national or international private interests seeking benefits without costs.

6.2 Improved Information as a Primary Requirement

Such state planning needs a much improved Labour Market Information System. An enabling employment strategy will have problems of predicting the final impact of policies, and will be much more aware of the likelihood of policy avoidance, evasion, defiance and distortion. The policy will recognise complex patterns of resource deficiencies at the household level, including time, energy, fixed assets, financial and credit inflows, education and training. The strategy will have to be based upon experiments in flexible package approaches with built-in on-going monitoring and evaluation rather than on rigid blueprints to be mechanically implemented.

An improved information network must include surveys designed to be superior to current surveys in terms of measurement and sampling accuracy and policy relevance (including becoming available in good time for policy decisions). Studies by Fareedy (1990), Irfan (1990), Kazi (1990) have indicated chronic deficiencies in current labour market data collection which cannot be allowed to continue on the basis of inertia or untested claims of errors being consistent. In this context there is a need for more interaction between policy makers and the research community. Major ministries like Agriculture, Industry, Education and Defence should include employment and human resource development in strengthened research wings. Their major functions should include the (i) identification of employment and human resource development issues in the sector (ii) formulation of the issues into research projects (iii) commissioning the research from experienced public or private organisations (iv) presentation of the research findings in a manner which informs policy makers fully on the complexity of the situation in a policy relevant context.

The Planning Commission needs to strengthen its own research capability in the employment and human resource development area. The economy should not be conceptualised as a collection of different economic sectors but through a micro-economic, household level aspect which will allow for incorporation in state planning of economic and social actions and interactions within and between households. Both the National Manpower Commission and the studies for this Project have made specific recommendations for improving the Labour Market Information System in terms of measurement methodology, sampling frames, periodicity, and institutional responsibilities. The next step is for the Federal Bureau of Statistics to convene an appraisal of these recommendations as a prelude to rapid implementation.

6.3 The Significance of Larger Scale Employing Units in Training for Human Resource Development

The existing Labour Market Information System probably significantly underestimates direct employment in larger scale units, especially in manufacturing. In any case, the priorities for such units in the 1990s will be to survive in the face of increasing international competition and use labour more productively. Increasing labour productivity is important everywhere in agriculture even if the rate of mechanisation is reduced.

Introduction of higher value added crops as suggested by the National Commission on Agriculture (NCA) and supported by the National Manpower Commission may have a role to play. But the existing commercially viable base is very small and development would entail a large amount of investment on the NCA's own calculations. Thus given these large overhead costs, it is not clear what the cost per additional job, especially in storage and distribution, would be in the NCA proposed shift towards fruits, vegetables and livestock.

The situation in large scale manufacturing units is even more unclear in terms of the implications of increasing numbers of people employed per unit. Researchers may have been using one third underestimates of existing employment in such units (System (Pvt.) Ltd. 1990). But there is little evidence that workers, whatever their number, are being employed in an internationally competitive manner in terms of physical productivity and quality of output.

What is more important than numbers employed per unit of fixed capital at this time is that the easy availability of imported machines and equipment through aid and trade have tended to blunt initiatives for innovation within Pakistan.

Technological development which is relevant to Pakistan could benefit greatly from technical worker initiatives. A basis for larger scale production and further sophistication in technology developed by specialists in Pakistan production units and universities needs to be developed in the 1990s.

Pakistan has not evolved a technology development environment in large scale units and today has an educational system ill-equipped for technological innovation. Kemal (1990) and Lee (1990) documented this problem of a human resource development gap at technical worker and specialist levels. The resulting recommendations are uniform in terms of setting a new orientation for technical and scientific education in Pakistan:

(a) Science and technology must receive special attention and priority resources at all levels in the education system, with external courses at advanced levels where appropriate.

(b) All technical and vocational education (including all engineering students) must involve workplace placements on actual work sites, parallel to placements in hospitals for student doctors.

(c) All technical and vocational education must involve potential employers of students in design and evaluation.

(d) Joint-venture technological Research and Development initiatives should be encouraged between production units and university researchers.

To enable such developments, state planners should experiment with a variety of ways to fund training in co-operation with the private sector, including those recommended by the National Manpower Commission, to finance expansion and introduce much more real accountability to employers and flexibility into public sector training. Large scale employing units in the public sector (which accounts for about half of total large scale unit regular wage and salary employment) are going to continue to be heavily constrained by a tight macro-economic situation. The combination of government budgetary deficit and international balance of payments deficit threatening to increase domestic price inflation and dependency on conditional international finance, will leave any government of Pakistan with very little room for manoeuvre to expand public sector employment in the foreseeable future.

The increasing contrast between the security of households with public sector employees and the insecurity of many of those without such employment will further encourage a mutual alienation, distrust, and hostility which will further erode any genuine sense of public service. Radical reform of the civil service, including a movement away from the Westminster model to more open forms of both popular and de-regulated market accountability, would encourage greater confidence among the mass of the population without destroying the principle of a fairly treated, adequately rewarded, public service.

In the narrow context of employment promotion a major failure has been the non-assessment of sustainability and consequences of crash programmes taken up as short term measures. This symptomatic treatment often tends to postpone and delay the emergence of the real problems, which then emerge later with added intractability and complexity. Decisions on education, length of job search, and migration are especially vulnerable to unrealistic or faulty signals emitted by the labour market, in the wake of such crash programmes. The public sector will continue to be a large scale purchaser and as such should use its purchasing power in a manner sensitive to both labour intensity in production of purchased items and the working conditions under which they were produced, especially health and safety and worker representation. Not only should the public sector be a best practice employer but also use its considerable purchasing power to encourage best practices in the private sector. A study of the construction industry by Zahid (1990) does indicate that the pattern of priorities of the public sector in the Seventh Plan for that sector is compatible with a significant employment gain, compared to the pre-existing pattern.

6.4 Small Scale Units as the Focus of Employment Generation

The focus of enabling employment generation tends to be on small scale units. The assumption behind this focus is that individuals and households frustrated in other directions will see opportunities for small scale unit development and plan to take initiatives, requiring for implementation appropriate, timely and limited state planned resources.

Sources of the dynamism and vibrancy of the broadly defined "informal" sector need to be clearly understood. Nearly all the commerce, most of the construction, a significant share of the transport and sizeable fraction of services are located in the informal sector. It must be clearly understood that their growth is mostly demand determined. There can be various sources of demand such as growth in the commodity producing sector, public expenditure or extraneous factors such as remittances, but for such activities especially, macro-economic policy enabling growing domestic effective demand by poorer consumers is important.

The situation is different in manufacturing where opportunities for direct linking between large scale and small scale units exist. Project surveys and studies (Aftab 1990 and Nadvi 1990) suggest at this time development of the small scale manufacturing sector depends on the growth in the income level of poorer sections of society and is taking the form of proliferation of units rather than expansion and deepening of existing units.

The pattern of existing small-scale industry in Pakistan has been immensely affected by the development of mass- production and mass-consumption industries on a world scale and in Pakistan. The basis for local handicraft and cottage activities serving local rural communities has been technically and economically undermined.

It is possible that some activities using primarily local inputs and labour to produce for local consumers may continue to survive and may benefit from appropriate technology upgrading, especially in areas where cash incomes are rising due to agricultural development or increased remittances. However, the cash income elasticity of demand with rising incomes is unlikely to favour locally produced items. Also, competing in terms of price while repaying loans for even simple equipment will be difficult. Nevertheless, some joint public sector/private sector expenditure on Research and Development of appropriate equipment may be justified on a mixture of social and commercial grounds.

It is more realistic to talk about the expansion of traditional crafts where highly specialised labour skills or an unusual natural resource base produce articles attractive to distant higher income consumers. Such opportunities have probably already been identified by private sector commercial entrepreneurs. In such cases, a responsibility falls upon the state to ensure these commercial entrepreneurs behave in a non-exploitative fashion, ensuring a fair share of rewards goes to the artisans, their skills are developed and the natural resource base is maintained.

Government inspection of contractual conditions and advice on forming cooperatives is appropriate given the typical vulnerability of rural artisan groups. A private sector (including tourism interests) and public sector joint programme to locate, develop and monitor specialist rural skills and resources could be a valuable component of a rural small-scale industry development strategy.

But more generally, the development of all small-scale industry, with its highly desirable employment effects, will depend on finding linkages with growing, profitable, larger scale enterprises on a branch, subsidiary or sub-contracting basis. Such linkages can be technically upstream (providing inputs) or downstream (utilising outputs) of large-scale industry or agriculture.

Studies of dynamic small-scale industries in urban and peri-urban areas in several countries have brought out their close linkages with large-scale industry. Such small-scale enterprises can operate upstream of one or two much larger enterprises through producing a specialised item or in an upstream/downstream role by engaging in part-assembly or fully downstream in undertaking a finishing role.

In most cases, such linkages are only cost-effective if small-scale and large-scale units are in close proximity. Industrial decentralisation of large-scale units often will be required to stimulate the development of near-by small-scale industrial units. Rural small-scale industrialisation would be a by-product of rural large-scale industrialisation. Consequent government policy would then seek to combine development of transport and energy infrastructure in rural areas, with regulations guiding location of plants, and possible minimal subsidies for economically sub-optimal location of plants.

However, such a government-enabled approach may not be necessary in all cases if the private sector could be persuaded to adopt a voluntary code to recognise that the social costs of urban agglomeration inevitably appear as private sector costs which could be reduced by each enterprise seeking to achieve some decentralisation with respect to new investment. The following series of questions for all investment projects might be included in such a code:

(a) Can the whole investment be made in a rural area?

(b) Can the whole investment be made in a rural area with the removal of an infrastructure constraint?

(c) Can the activities resulting from the investment be broken down into a number of sub-processes (in series and in parallel) capable of being operated and controlled independently at a distance with different requirements for infrastructure and labour skills/work conditions?

(d) Can any of these sub-processes be located in rural areas at an acceptable cost distance from the main plant with or without some minimal infrastructure improvement?

The development of rural small-scale industry through linkages with agriculture, fisheries and forestry development appears to offer great potential. Possibilities are growing of upstream technical linkages through input provision and downstream technical linkages through processing. In addition, infrastructure development in terms of transport and energy aimed at developing agriculture, fisheries or forestry can also serve rural small-scale industry. Finally, growing incomes from primary sector activities can provide part of the demand for some rural industrialisation.

In practice, a good deal of what is commonly included in rural small-scale industrialisation could almost be regarded as primary rather than secondary sector activity and displacing domestic employment rather than creating new employment. Poultry and other small livestock rearing and marketing, grain and oil milling, fish preserving and marketing, saw-milling are examples of such rural activities totally integrated with the primary sector. Such activities are important in retaining value-added in rural areas when volumes of output have significantly increased and may have a role in decreasing domestic drudgery.

Successful international examples of rural industrialisation in China and India were largely built through local enterprise building on a dynamic local agricultural base with relatively easy access to an urban centre. In such cases, agricultural surpluses appear to have been relatively easily converted into input provision and output processing whether those surpluses were controlled by commercial farmers or collective communes. There was little need for public sector or non-agricultural private sector resources to be put directly into such agro-industrialisation.

Overall therefore, there exist a range of possible roads to rural small-scale industrialisation. Most rural localities will need an element of greater rural industrialisation and its associated employment if sufficient productive activity is to be available for the growing labour force. But the precise road and the form of external support required for a particular locality will differ greatly and sensitivity is needed to specific potentials.

Market forces left to their own devices will sensitively guide large-scale commercial industrial, and agricultural private sector enterprises into rural, large and small-scale industry to develop and exploit the most profitable activities in promising locations. Greater social responsibility in the private sector could extend this range.

The public sector may have a role in ensuring cost-effective efficiency of such developments on a profit-sharing joint venture, or loan basis. The government also has a regulatory role in ensuring an equitable distribution of benefits. But the government and public sector also have a vital wider responsibility for enabling bottom-up, grassroots initiatives to be developed independent of the interests of large-scale enterprises.

The outreach of large-scale enterprises into all small-scale industries is important and greater recognition of responsibility for such outreach in the large-scale private sector is needed if individual hardship and social costs of growing unemployment, underemployment and non-productive rural- urban migration are to be avoided. But even a more enlightened large-scale private sector would still omit many micro-scale opportunities requiring a sensitive understanding of local resource, labour or market availability.

Public sector assistance to bring such opportunities to fruition needs to be aware of all the potential constraints and offer a package tailored to the specific situation drawing on the experience of the Small Scale Industries' Corporations. Also assistance may need to continue in varying forms over several years if the enterprise is to survive the different problems of birth, infancy, childhood and adolescence.

In the first instance, the degrees of development of the initiator's product idea, proposed technology, and perceived market are bound to be uneven and based on optimism rather than calculation. Building up neglected aspects and examining a range of scenarios is best done on a "single window" basis. Choices of technology and market are not independent of each other; a technology that produces at a cost that target consumers cannot afford is never appropriate. Fixed capital cost per job created should be used as a criterion to prioritise proposals but not imposed on any particular proposal so as to make it unable to survive economically.

Credit is almost invariably the central resource transfer and the terms on which it is given are critical policy choices. The lower the minimum security required and the higher the maximum proportion of fixed and working capital covered, the more accessible the facility to low income clients but the fewer the clients who will be covered by a given fund. In practice, the total funds made available should be decided through continuing monitoring and evaluation of active and pipeline initiatives and priority given to cost-effective employment creation in promising new lines of activity where private sector support is lacking.

A person who has a feasible idea and necessary collateral does not necessarily have managerial, accounting and marketing skills. Yet in the early stages of an enterprise, this individual will probably have to play all these roles. Continuing advice and timely training should be available in the package.

Similarly the initiator may not have technical knowledge of equipment and materials or access to resources for modifying and maintaining equipment. Technical support in advisory and practical forms is a desirable item in the package.

Finally, recruitment, training, conditions of employment and labour relations (including issues of gender and age mix, hours and seasonality of work, wage and piece rates, health and safety, grievances and discipline) may be areas requiring advice and mediation.

The concept of an enabling package offered over a period of time with a range of potential elements is intended to maximise the possibility of success of vulnerable, valuable enterprises; enterprises vulnerable due to factors of inexperience, remoteness, non-specialisation, and valuable due to factors of productive employment creation and income generation in new lines of activity. But the package's very comprehensiveness for individual cases limits its ability to cover large numbers of cases and restricts the number and sectoral orientation of centres from which the package can be offered.

Thus the package needs to be targeted geographically and possibly sectorally. Placing Industrial Support Centres in areas of industrialisation potential increases the probability of success but risks supporting activities that the private sector would have undertaken anyway. At the current experimental stage of enabling small scale industrialisation in Pakistan, there is probably room for both independent private sector and public sector supported activity to develop in relatively favourable localities looking towards transfer of successful experience to less favourable areas in the future.

The role of public sector support would be to take higher risks in terms of sectors and socio-economic background of initiators to widen experience of small scale industrialisation. Attempts should be made to attract such initiators from those employed in large scale units and thus with experience and skills which make them more likely to succeed in a new business, not concentrated on those without skills and work experience.

6.5 Improving Access to Productive Economic Activity for Women

One of the prime objectives of an enabling employment and human resource development strategy is to focus state planners attention on those whose human resource potential is most neglected by the existing planning process and undervalued by market forces. In Pakistan, as in many societies, this objective turns the state planning focus on women.

Women face a variety of problems in entering and moving in all areas of economic activity. The specific problems will vary depending on each woman's particular circumstances which may appear to make generalisation difficult. But, in essence, when facing the issue of all women's economic activity, we are facing the issue of the very meaning of development itself.

It is possible to base a concern with women in economic activity by arguing on human resource grounds that Pakistan operates with one hand tied behind its back in struggling for development while neglecting half its potential human resources. This argument implicitly accepts that the meaning of development is centred on increasing economic growth and/or reducing population growth and women in economic activity are only a means to those ends. This argument can be made to appear less instrumentalist if it is extended to include women's right to share proportionately in the benefits of per capita economic growth.

An alternative definition of development starts from the position that the essential meaning of development is about increasing opportunities for all citizens of Pakistan to express their positive, creative and productive talents as they choose. From this perspective, women having choices in economic activities is an end in itself not just a means. Just as health, literacy and choice over number of children can be seen as rights rather than merely instruments to raise per capita economic growth rates.

The first "instrumentalist" view has been made fashionable by IMF arguments that people are "human capital" valued in the market. As a logical consequence, policy should be validated by appeal, qualitative or quantitative, to the existence of net discounted gains in the present value of per capita GNP. That view is not accepted here, fundamentally on the foundation of choosing a different principle for defining development, and technically because market-based calculations in conditions of existing extreme inequalities in power will tend to give low market values to the activities of the powerless.

The second "developmentalist" view argues that women have a fundamental right of access to all economic activities on an equal basis with men without the need for justification on economic or population growth grounds, though extending this fundamental right may well result in higher per capita GNP growth.

The principle advanced here is that Pakistani women have an equal right with Pakistani men to seek to improve their quality of life by acting in well-informed concert with others (family, neighbours, workmates, fellow-citizens) to achieve mutually agreed goals. It is argued here that a twin track strategic approach is appropriate both to gain greater recognition and equal treatment for women already economically active, and also, equality of access with men for women who wish to enter or re-enter economic activity.

An enabling strategy for all women requires advance on a broad front so that gains in one area, worthwhile in their own right, will reinforce and encourage gains in other areas. Gains for women who are engaged in higher status, higher public profile economic activities will encourage women engaged in lower status economic activity to make claims against gender discrimination. Gains for the many women who are already economically active will encourage other women to enter economic activity if they wish. Such an approach will involve conflict in lines of economic activity where women have been employed simply for their high exploitability, but there is no evidence that such employers will find it economical to substitute men or machines for women at the margin and that losses of employment will result.

In terms of the development of specific programmes and projects in a strategic framework for all women in Pakistan, it may be useful to think in terms of a continuum, whose range encompasses all women's experiences and aspirations. At one end, the continuum must have meaning to a woman who never attended school and feels unable to venture far from her house, but who wishes to take a step towards literacy, an improved domestic environment, and possible "secluded" economic activity. At the other end, it must offer improved career development prospects to a professionally trained woman, whose promotion is hindered by gender factors.

The strategic challenge is to provide a series of manageable steps between the two ends of the continuum, so that in principle a woman can move from one end to the other or stop at any point she chooses. Three necessary prior, general conditions for the strategy are that all upper age bars in programmes and projects be removed, attendance timings be flexible, and that formal education requirements be the minimum necessary for the activity. Removal of age bars and flexible timing will allow entry and exit from economic activity to fit with "breaks" when a woman wishes to prioritise domestic activities. If formal education requirements are not set to ration out scarce opportunities, then any needed rationing can be done on explicit criteria aimed at achieving a mix of women participants from a variety of backgrounds.

Five steps in the continuum are outlined below and examples of activities currently to be found in Pakistan are given for each step:

(a) The locality-centred environmental health and literacy-centred home-schooling projects for girls and women in Baldia can be seen as representing a first step on the continuum. Relieving the domestic burden on women is crucial to this step and can involve releasing time and energy through, either, reducing the effort needed, e.g. to maintain the household in basic water and fuel supplies, or, increasing time and energy available by reducing time and energy losses due to sickness of the woman herself or those for whom she has primary responsibility as carer.

The released time and energy may be used to undertake more economic activity. If so, the choice of economic activities and the conditions under which economic activity is undertaken are likely to improve if the woman is literate at least to the point of being able to understand written instructions and enter into written contracts. The Baldia twin track approach of making time and energy available and increasing literacy as a basic requirement to gain greater income in a home/local community setting is to be commended as a model.

(b) Where the first step has a firm foundation, then a second step can be constructed. The women-oriented elements of the Orangi Pilot Project (OPP) offer excellent examples of this second step. Building on the commercially viable existing activities of women in their homes (a much more common phenomenon in Pakistan than official statistics suggest), the OPP has encouraged women to cut out "middle-men" and improve their contractual relationship as well as offering access to appropriate new technology.

Choice between working at home or in a small-scale workplace has been created, as well as choice of being a piece-rate worker or manager/entrepreneur. The OPP is an example of stressing commercial viability and technical upgrading of production of unglamorous items for use in mass production. These are crucial aspects in the second step, too many women's income generation efforts have attempted to produce frivolous consumer items using laborious techniques which have not had the quality to find a worthwhile price. For instance, embroidery is an excellent, creative leisure activity but has been a dark dead-end for the lives, and eyesight, of poor working women on a world scale for centuries. But even direct production for higher income consumers can be successful if a hard-headed commercial approach is adopted as appears to be the case with the Behbud NGO toy producing projects in Rawalpindi.

(c) In situations where women are clearly economically active outside the home, such as in many rural areas, the next step in the continuum becomes available for construction. The Agha Khan Rural Support Project (AKRSP) offers an example of what can be done. The AKRSP initially identified, with local women themselves, the women's existing pattern of activities in the project areas in rural north Pakistan, including the economic activities of vegetable production, live-stock management, and orchard management.

In full consultation with women's groups, improved access to credit and appropriate improved inputs was created, and local women were trained in administering the inputs. Reducing time and energy needed for domestic activities was also an objective. While respecting cultural norms in the specific communities involved in the AKRSP (which is relatively unproblematic for this particular Foundation operating in this locality), the approach appears to have stressed women's collective, co-operative organisational development alongside, and not subordinated to, the development of new economic activities with significantly improved, self-managed technologies.

(d) Each step outlined so far has involved relatively informal, relatively self-employed, and relatively non-mechanised technology. For women's economic activity to move beyond these characteristics will require opportunities to take formal training in formal, employable, higher technology skills. Out of the host of recent training initiatives, only a few stand up to scrutiny with respect to these three criteria.

The women's polytechnics in Lahore and Karachi may offer promising examples in courses offering training in electronic equipment technology, technical design/drawing skills, and secretarial skills, as well as higher technology garment production training. Applicants face barriers of age and Matriculation qualification requirements, but, on the positive side placements with local employers appear to have been easy to find.

The importance of close links to local employers for all activities on this step, up to and including formal arrangements for "sandwich courses"/work experience placements/day releases apprenticeships, cannot be overemphasised. This principle also applies to training for men, but has special significance for women whose employment environment needs some specific planning.

(e) The final step in the continuum is access to formal, full-time education places for degree level qualifications in the professions and advancement within the professions to the highest levels of management. Here again, the value of in-course work placements should not be underestimated and the final employment of women graduates should be a matter of institutional concern. Different professions face women with different access problems to courses and employment and advancement, and none can be cited as offering an unambiguous best-practice model at this time.

Engineering has chronic quantitative and qualitative demand and supply side deficiencies. Medical schools would probably offer more places to women if, originally protective, discriminatory quotas were now removed and places were offered purely on merit. All other degree courses could probably improve access for women by a mixture of some additional physical provision and much attitudinal change.

Nursing and teaching, especially the sciences, need matching supply side expansion of both training and jobs. Steady expansion is required which is qualitatively sensitive to the need to achieve a better urban and rural balance and develop local environmental sensitivity and community women's leadership skills in these key professions.

To make access to the professions a real prospect for the many women whose formal schooling was prematurely stopped, it is important that distance learning opportunities be increased and phased formal assessment instituted up to a level acceptable as entrance qualifications for tertiary education. The Allama Iqbal

Open University already possesses useful experience in distance learning provision for women. "Updating" courses for women who have taken a career "break" to take the lioness' share of domestic responsibilities are also relevant in this respect.

Overall, constructing a continuum of opportunities in Pakistan will involve more women meeting more Pakistan federal and provincial state institutions in a wide variety of roles. But meeting such institutions involves a double problem for women which makes the general form of the contact itself a matter for policy, in addition to the specific content.

Firstly, a majority of women are illiterate and have little experience of bureaucratic culture and procedures, which are heavily dependent on written records and direct, classificatory questions dismissive of the particulars of individual cases. Many men also have this problem and find state institutions unapproachable. But women have the additional problem that the state institutions are literally "manned" and involve cross-gender contact between strangers.

Something could be achieved by training men in institutions, or particular sections of institutions, with which women are expected to come into contact, in gender neutrality. But, even if such training were successful in changing key men's attitudes and behaviour, this would not remove the reluctance of many women to place themselves in any relationship with a male stranger (for perfectly understandable reasons given the attitudes of sections of Pakistan society and the current state of the law).

Three ways to bring women and state institutions together are the subjects of active experiment in Pakistan at this time:

(a) Separate women designated institutions, such as the Ministry for Women Development and the Women Development Bank, have a flagship role and ensure representation of a women's interest in higher level fora. But the prospects of establishing a network across a sufficient range of services in enough localities to offer a parallel "Women's" state is remote. Even if constructed the cost-effectiveness would be dubious. Also, to give an institution the title "Women's" does not mean that all employees will be women (and perhaps it is not in women's wider interests that so-named institutions should become "ghettos") and so the fundamental problem of "manning" may not be resolved.

(b) A second form of experiment involves the opening of women's "windows" in general "line" institutions staffed by women. Such facilities are claimed currently to be offered in the Sukkur Employment Office and the Sindh Commissioner's Office. This approach does meet the immediate problem of eliminating cross-gender contact for clients as well as increasing employment of women in the institutions adopting the approach. Much could be done in this direction by all regulatory and development institutions having contact with the public. Such "windows" need not be offering services on special terms for women, the primary aim would be to give women equal access on equal terms.

(c) But given that the second approach will only be instituted unevenly across institutions and locations in practice and may never be universal, given questions of cost-effectiveness at small service outlets and problems in practice of employing isolated women workers in remote locations, there is a need for development of "advocacy" skills which will translate women's expressed needs into targeted claims on institutions and present and progress- chase those claims through the institutions.

The development of advocacy is a role which NGOs are frequently interested in playing. But NGO coverage is itself uneven and if policies are to reach all women then there is need for state action to ensure there are women "change agents" available to all communities assisting advocacy as and when required.

A strategic enabling approach provides a framework for action to widen choice and improve access for all women with respect to productive economic activity. The strategy gives a potential role to many federal and provincial government institutions, as well as NGOs.

The strategy encourages widespread, systematic experiments in women-directed, affordable and sustainable, local and national development programmes. In aggregate, these experiments would aim to diminish domestic drudgery, reduce illiteracy, generate incomes, fight middle-men exploitation, develop appropriate technology, open up formal high- technology training opportunities in co-operation with larger employers, and place women alongside men at the top of every profession and organisation. Much needs to be done in facilitating advocacy, which could include access to legal aid, counselling, and resources for women workers in trades union development.

There is an immediate policy need to institute a national advisory appraisal and monitoring and evaluation capacity for these experiments developing widely applicable techniques and sensitive performance indicators. The obvious place for this capacity to be located is in the Ministry for Women Development.

In terms of providing an environment for strategy development, it is vital that immediate action be taken in:

(a) Improving data collection procedures, especially in the coming population census, to reflect adequately the actual lives of women in Pakistan;

(b) Removing de jure and de facto discriminatory legislation and regulations, extending protective labour legislation to cover casual, contract and home-workers to give a legal basis for advocacy;

(c) Providing material incentives to all employers to provide workplace transportation, childcare provision, and equal access to training and career development for men and women which could be associated with reclaimable levies;

(d) Building training capacity for a cadre of Women's Development Officers with a broad curriculum and deploying them to work in institutional and community, urban and rural settings as planners, implementers, inspectors and advocates. The Seventh Five Year Plan has recognised this need in proposing to train and deploy six thousand female Women's Development Officers (Pakistan Seventh Five Year Plan, 1988-93, page 255).

6.6 An Enabling Strategy and Reducing Poverty and Contributing to Long-Run Environmental Sustainability

Enabling more women to become more productively economically active is likely to be a major contribution of an enabling approach to employment and human resource development state planning and reducing poverty. Many women may continue to be only marginally economically active but they will play a vital role in supporting and, in turn, receive securer consumption rights through mothers, sisters and daughters as well as fathers, brothers and sons.

In addition, more education and more productive employment for all women should encourage reduced fertility which is the key to a sustainable environment in Pakistan. The National Manpower Commission gives the highest priority to reducing the population growth rate. The current crude birth rate is believed to be still between 41 and 43 per 1000 population, which suggests no significant decline over the past four decades.

Pakistan's data and research studies are indicative of a continuous rise in age at marriage from 17.9 in 1951, to 20.0 years in 1972. The 1981 Census yielded Singulate Mean Age at Marriage of 20.8 years. Thus a gain of three years has been achieved during the three decades. In parallel, the celibacy rate during the same period rose from 3.8 per cent to 17.7 per cent among women up to 21 years of age. But the effect of this rising age at marriage appears to have been countered by a "catching up" phenomenon so that women who marry late tend to end up with the same completed family size as those who marry at early ages. Therefore policies which tend to restrict employment opportunities to girls and older women will not necessarily reduce overall fertility.

On the level of contraceptive use, data are also hardly encouraging. Recent evidence provided by Pakistan's Contraceptive Prevalence Survey measured the percentage of current users to be 9.1 percent, a low level by South Asian standards. The characteristics of contraceptive users show little discernible change over time. The typical user female already has five living children with six or more children ever born. The average age of contraceptive user female falls in the age bracket of 30-34 years. It is policy aiming at productive employment for women in their twenties which is most likely to raise the demand for contraception in the peak fertility years.

6.7 The Political Agenda

An open political system must admit claims for special treatment by all self-identified interest groups in society. Pakistan is very rich in such groups and such claims. Regional, religious, and ethnic characteristics form strong bases for disruptive mobilisation. In Pakistan in the 1990s, employment pressures with closely associated, but independent, experiences of poverty and social rejection will continue to feed into competing claims for political attention. The political culture of Pakistan (but not only Pakistan) is not one of tolerance with respect to frustrated claims and many groups possess the will and the means to meet frustration with open and covert militant defiance of the writ of the government.

Opportunistic attempts to meet claims as they arise is unlikely to produce a stable political situation. Rather government should set out clear strategic priorities and performance criteria for the decade and direct all policies towards them and firmly resist special interest claims that detract from those priori-ties. The authors of this book advocate that state planning to enable the currently most powerless people to have more choice over their employment and more opportunity to develop their human resources should have priority as a development objective.

References

Abbasi, Nasreen & Irfan, M: *Socio-Economic Effects of International Migration on the Families Left Behind*, PLM Report No.7, PIDE, Islamabad, 1983.

Aftab, Khalid: *Increasing Employment, Unemployment and Underemployment*, Planning Division, Government of Pakistan, Islamabad, 1990.

Ahmed, Viqar and Amjad, Rashid: *The Management of Pakistan's Economy: 1947-82*. Oxford University Press, Karachi, 1984.

Alam, Iqbal et al. *"Fertility Levels, Trends and Differentials in Pakistan : Evidence from the Population Labour Force and Migration Survey 1979-80,"* PIDE, Islamabad, 1983.

Amjad, Rashid (ed): *To The Gulf and Back: Studies on the Economic Impact of Asian Migration*, ARTEP/ILO, New Delhi, 1989.

Anwar A.A. : *Problems of Unemployed Educated Manpower*. The Board of Economic Enquiry, Punjab, Pakistan, 1973.

ARTEP/ILO: *Labour Market Adjustment To Emigration in Pakistan*, Bangkok, 1986.

Applied Economics Research Centre, University of Karachi: *Quantification of Unemployment Among Educated Youth in Pakistan*, Karachi, 1989.

ARTEP/ILO: *A Report in the Rural Industrialisation Program of Punjab Small Industries Corporation, Pakistan*, New Delhi, 1989.

ARTEP/ILO: *Employment Generation Through Rural Small Industries in Pakistan: Potential and Constraints*, New Delhi, 1989.

ARTEP/ILO: *Mid-Review of the Employment and Labour Market Situation in Pakistan During the Sixth Five Year Plan (1983-88)*, New Delhi, March 1988.

ARTEP/ILO: *Pakistan Employment and Manpower Strategies and Policies Project (Pak/88/007) Interim Report*, New Delhi, 1989

Aslam, Naheed: *Wages, Employment and Labour Productivity in the Manufacturing Sector of Punjab*, PIDE, Islamabad, 1982.

Burney, Nadeem: *A Macro-Economic Analysis of the Impact of Worker's Remittances From the Middle East on Pakistan's Economy*, ARTEP/ILO, New Delhi, 1988.

Chaudhry, M.G: "The State and Development of Rural Industries in Pakistan" In *Development and Diversification of Rural Industries in Asia. Edited by Swapna Mukhopadhyay and Chee Ping Line*, APDC Kuala Lumpur, Malaysia, 1985.

Child, F.C. and Kaneda, H: "Links to the Green Revolution : A Study of Small-Scale Agriculturally Related Industry in Pakistan's Punjab." *Economic Development and Cultural Change*. Vol. 23, Chicago, 1975.

Eckert, Jerry: *Rural Labour in Punjab*, Planning and Development Department, Govt. of the Punjab, Lahore, July 1972.

Elahi, Mahboob and M. Jameel Khan: *Rural Labour Market with Special Reference to Hired Labour in Pakistan's Punjab in Hired Labour and Rural Labour Markets in Asia*. ARTEP/ILO, New Delhi, 1986.

Emmay Associates: *Evaluation of Technical & Vocational Education System and its Impact on Manpower Development in Pakistan*, Planning Division, Government of Pakistan, Islamabad, 1991.

Ercelawn, Aly: "Income Inequality in Pakistan: A study of Sample Villages",*Pakistan Journal of Applied Economics*. Summer, 1984.

Fareedy, Fareed Ahmad: *Improved System for Monitoring Employment in Large Scale Manufacturing, Small Scale Manufacturing, Construction and in the Public Sector*, Planning Division, Government of Pakistan, Islamabad, 1990.

Federal Bureau of Statistics: *Survey of Distributive Trades & Services, 1984-85* (Rural Urban), Islamabad, 1989.

Federal Bureau of Statistics: *"Survey of Mechanised Road Transport, Karachi 1981. Lahore 1981-82, Peshawar 1981-82. Rawalpindi, 1981-82*, Islamabad, 1985.

Federal Bureau of Statistics: *Monthly Statistical Bulletin*, Islamabad, December, 1989.

Ghayur, Sabur: *Unemployment in Pakistan—An Overview and Future Prospects*, Pakistan Manpower Institute, Islamabad, 1987.

Gilani, I et al.: *Labour Migration from Pakistan to the Middle East and its Impact on the Domestic Economy*, PIDE, Islamabad, 1981.

GOP/Finance Division: *Economic Survey 1986-87*, Islamabad, 1987

GOP/Finance Division: *Economic Survey 1988-89*, Islamabad, 1989.

GOP/Ministry of Labour: *Labour Market Adjustment To Emigration In Pakistan*, Islamabad, 1986.

GOP/Population Division: *Pakistan's Contraceptive Prevalence Survey 1984-85*, Islamabad, 1988.

Gulbrandsen Odd: *Pakistan's Labour Market Problems: A Computer Simulation*, Planning Division, Government of Pakistan, 1990.

Guisinger, Hicks and Pilvin: *Wages and Relative Prices*, mimeo, 1977.

Guisinger & Irfan M: "Real Wages of Industrial Workers In Pakistan: 1954 To 1970," *PDR*, Islamabad, Winter 1974.

Guisinger & Irfan M: "Pakistan's Informal Sector," *Journal of Development Studies*. Vol. 16, No.4, London, July 1980.

Hafeez, Sabeeha: *Women in Industry in Pakistan*, 2 Volumes, Women's Division, Government of Pakistan, Islamabad, 1989.

Herman & Irfan M: *Employment and Unemployment in Pakistan: Some Simulations for the Year 2003 — Paper Presented in the Sixth Annual General Meeting of PSDE*, PIDE, Islamabad, 1990.

Hussain, Akmal: *Strategic Issues in Pakistan's Economic Policy*. Progressive Publishers Ltd., Lahore, 1988.

Hussain Akmal : *Labour Absorption in the Agricultural Sector*, Planning Division, Government of Pakistan, Islamabad, 1990.

ILO: *Impact of Return Migration on Domestic Employment in Pakistan: A Preliminary Analysis*. Geneva, April, 1984.

ILO: *Report to the Government of Pakistan Sectoral Review Mission (July-August 1986)*. Geneva, 1987.

Iqbal, Munawar and Khan M. Faheem: *Economic Implication of the Return Flow of Immigrants from the Middle East: A Preliminary Study*, PIDE, Research Report No. 132, Islamabad 1981.

Irfan, M: *Consequences of Outmigration on the Domestic Labour Market: A Case Study of Pakistan.* ARPLA Research Studies, Bangkok. 1983.

Irfan, M. & Kemal, A.R: "Employment and Manpower Projections for the Sixth Plan Period" in *Employment and Structural Change in Pakistan's Economy — Issues for the Eighties*, Proceedings of an ILO-ARTEP Seminar, Bangkok, April 1983.

Irfan, M: *"Poverty and Household Demographic Behaviour In Pakistan — Insights From PLM Survey 1979" (Project Report No. 11)*, PIDE, Islamabad, 1985.

Irfan M: *Migration and Development in Pakistan: Some Selected Issues.* PIDE, Islamabad, 1986.

Irfan, M: *Economic Development and Labour Use in Pakistan 1947-87.* PIDE, Islamabad, 1988, mimeo.

Irfan, M: "Outmigration and Labour Market Adjustment in Pakistan" In *Monitoring Labour Markets.* ARPLA (ILO), Bangkok, 1985.

Irfan, M : *Poverty and Household Demographic Behaviour in Pakistan - insights From PLM Survey 1979* (Studies in Population, Labour Force and Migration Project Report No.11), PIDE, Islamabad, 1985.

Irfan, M: *The Determinants of Female Labour Force Participation, PLM Research Report No. 5*, PIDE, Islamabad, 1983.

Irfan, M & Arif G.M: *Landlessness in Pakistan—A Preliminary Investigation*, PIDE, 1985.

Irfan, M: "Poverty, Class Structure and Household Demographic Behaviour in Rural Pakistan, In *Population Growth and Poverty in Rural South Asia*, edited by Gerry Rodgers, SAGE Publications, New Delhi, 1989.

Irfan M. et al: *Migration Patterns in Pakistan: Preliminary Results from the PLM Survey, 1979*, PIDE, Islamabad, 1983.

Irfan, M. & Ahmed M: "Real Wages in Pakistan: Structure and Trends 1970-84." *The Pakistan Development Review.* Islamabad, Autumn-Winter, 1985.

Irfan, M. and Amjad, R: "Poverty in Rural Pakistan" In *Poverty in Rural Asia.* Edited by A.R. Khan and Eddy Lee. ILO (ARTEP), Bangkok, 1988.

Irfan, M. assisted by Younus, M: *Measurement of Employment and Unemployment in Pakistan — A Methodological Survey* (also Manual of Instruction for Field Enumerators/Supervisors), Planning Division, GOP, 1990.

Irfan, M: "Effect of Unionzation, Product Market Concentration and Foreign Trade on Inter-Industry Wage structure," *Pakistan Development Review*, No. 1, Islamabad, Spring 1979.

Irfan, M: "Wages Employment and Trade Unions in Pakistan", *Pakistan Development Review*, No. 1 Islamabad, Spring 1982.

Jaffe A. J. and Stewart C. D.: *Manpower Resources and Utilization.* Wiley, 1951.

Jozefwicz A: *Unemployment among the Educated Youth*, Planning Division, GOP 1970.

Kazi, Shahnaz: *Special Problems of Women's Employment in Pakistan*, Planning Division, GOP, 1990.

Kazı, Shahnaz: *Domestic Impact of Remittances and Overseas Migration: Pakistan.* Asian Regional Programme on International Labour Migration, PIDE, Islamabad, 1987.

Kemal A.R : *Employment and Manpower Planning and Monitoring*, PIDE, Islamabad, June, 1989.

Kemal A.R : *Measures for Bringing About a Better Balance Between Supply and Demand for Major Professional/Skills Categories*, Planning Department, GOP, 1990.

Khan, A.R : "What has Been Happening to Reals Wages in Pakistan?" *Pakistan Development Review*, Islamabad, Autumn 1987.

Khan, Nighat Said: "Industrialisation, Culture and Women Workers in Pakistan", In Heyzer, Noeleen (ed), *Daughters in Industry*. Asian and Pacific Development Centre, Kuala Lumpur, Malaysia, 1988.

Khan, S.A. and Bilquees, F: *The Attitudes, Environment and Activities of Rural Women, a case study of Jhok Sayal*, PIDE, Islamabad, 1976.

Kibria, Ghulam: *Development Options: Muscle or Money*, Karachi, 1984.

Kibria, Ghulam: *Increasing Productivity and Employment Through Technological Upgradation in Cottage and Small Scale Industries*, Planning Division, GOP, 1990.

Lee, Mu Keun: *Technical/Vocational Education System*, Planning Division, GOP, 1990.

Malick, Susan: *Planning Income and Employment Generation for Rural Women — The Marketing Approach*, ILO, Geneva, 1985.

Malik, Mohammad Hussain: "Trends in Poverty in Pakistan: 1963/64 To 1984/85" *The Pakistan Development Review*, No.4, Islamabad, Winter 1988.

Mohiuddin, Y: *Female-Headed Households and Urban Poverty in Pakistan, Paper Presented at 13th Annual Meeting of Eastern Economic Association*, Washington, USA, 1987.

Moore, W.E: "The Exportability of the Labour Force Concept", *American Socio-Economic Review*, Washington, USA, Feb. 1953.

Nadvi, Khalid M: *Employment Generation Through Growth of Informal/ Small Scale Manufacturing in Urban Areas*, Planning Division, GOP, 1990.

Naseem, S.M.: *Underdevelopment, Poverty, and Inequality in Pakistan*, Vanguard Publications, Lahore, 1981.

National Institute of Population Studies: *Effects of Rapid Population Growth on Social and Economic Development ın Pakistan*. Islamabad, 1989.

National Manpower Commission: *Female Employment and Their Training needs, Study No. 1*, National Manpower Commission, GOP, Islamabad, 1989a.

National Manpower Commission: *Women's Employment and Training, Committee No. 8*, National Manpower Commission, GOP, Islamabad, 1989b.

National Mapower Commission: *An Agenda for Human Resource Development Policy and Employment in Pakistan—Advanced Draft of a Report*, National Manpower Commission, GOP, 1989c.

Planning Commission/GOP: *Seventh Five year Plan 1988-93 & Perspective Plan 1988-2003*. GOP, Islamabad, undated.

Rahman, Akhlaqur: *The Analysis of Relative Wage and Salary Structure in Pakistan*, Planning Commission, Islamabad, 1970.

Robinson, Warren C. & Nasreen Abbasi: "Under-Employment in Pakistan," *The Pakistan Development Review*. Islamabad, Winter 1979.

Ruud K: *Manpower and Educational Requirements of Pakistan*. Pakistan Planning Commission, Karachi, 1970.

Shima, Hira: *Hired Labour in Asia*, Institute of Developing Studies, Tokyo, 1980.

Standing, G: *Labour Force Participation and Development*, ILO, Geneva, 1978.

Systems (Pvt) Ltd: *Survey of Large Scale Manufacturing Enterprises—A Study of Contract Labour*, Planning Division, GOP, Islamabad, 1990.

Turnhaume, D.: *The Employment Problem in Less Developed Countries*, O.E.C.D. Papers, 1971.

Van Lent E: *Lahore Polytechnic Graduates Employment Survey Fourth Plan Research Papers No. 15*, Govt. of Punjab, Planning and Development Department, Lahore, March 1971.

Visaria Pravin: *Comparative Evaluation of the Concepts and Measures of Unemployment used in countries of Asian Region*. A paper presented at ESCAP/ILO Seminar on Employment and Unemployment, Bangkok, Jan. 1989.

Wizarat, S: "Inter-Industry Productivity Differentials in Pakistan's Large Scale Manufacturing Sector", *Singapore Economic Review*, Vol. XXXIII No.2, Singapore, October 1988.

Wizarat, Shahida and Zafar, Naeem ud Din : *Intra-Sectoral Productivity Differential : The Large-Scale Versus the Small-Scale Sector in Pakistan*, Applied Economics Research Centre, Karachi, 1989.

World Bank: *Pakistan Education Sector Strategy Review*, Washington, USA, 1988a.

World Bank: *Report on Employment Issues in Pakistan*, Washington, USA, 1988b.

World Bank: *Pakistan Employment Issues and Prospects*, Washington, USA, 1989a.

World Bank: *Women in Pakistan—An Economic and Social Strategy*, Washington USA, 1988b.

Zahid, Shahid: *Role of Construction Sector in Employment Generation*, Planning Division, GOP, Islamabad, 1990.

Annexe I

Tables from Project Rural Small Scale Industry Survey

TABLE 1

Rural Industry Male Workers

Code	Industry Major Group	Total Units		Total Male Workers							
				Irrigated				Rainfed			
		Irrigated	Rainfed	Mean	S.D	Mini-mum Value	Maxi-mum Value	Mean	S.D	Mini-mum Value	Maxi mum Value
		(1)	(2)	(3)	(4)	(5)	(6)	(7)	(8)	(9)	(10)
Total		426	174	3.30	6.50		107	3.08	5.84	1	76
37-38	Metal Industries	74	17	2.48	1.46	1	7	2.23	1.86	1	9
	Other Industries	352	157	3.47	7.11		107	3.17	6.11	1	76
3	Manufacturing	426	174	3.30	6.50		107	3.08	5.84	1	76
31	Manufacture of Food, Beverages and Tobacco	116	65	3.14	1.35	1	9	2.32	1.50	1	8
311-312	Food Manufacturing	108	64	3.24	1.86	1	9	2.29	1.50	1	8
3115	Manufacture of Vegetable and Inedible Animal Oils and Fats	15	12	3.20	1.75	1	8	1.91	1.44	1	6
31152	Vegetable Oils Except Hydrogenated Oils and Cotton Seed Oils	15	11	3.20	1.79	1	8	1.54	0.78	1	3
3116	Grain Milling and Products thereof	76	42	2.89	1.63	1	9	2.11	1.22	1	8
31162	Wheat and Grain Milling except Rice	72	42	2.86	1.85	1	8	2.11	1.22	1	8
3117	Manufacture of Bakery Products	13	7	4.76	1.84	2	8	4.14	2.03	2	7
314	Tobacco Manufacturing	8	1	1.87	1.05	1	4	4.00	—	4	4
32	Textile, Wearing Apparel and Leather Industries	65	21	2.58	3.10	—	20	1.80	1.14	1	5

Contd.

TABLE 1 (Contd.)
Rural Industry Male Workers

	Industry Major Group	Total Units		Total Male Workers							
				Irrigated				Rainfed			
		Irrigated	Rainfed	Mean	S.D	Minimum Value	Maximum Value	Mean	S.D	Minimum Value	Maximum Value
		(1)	(2)	(3)	(4)	(5)	(6)	(7)	(8)	(9)	(10)
320-321	Manufacture of Textiles	36	7	3.02	3.35	—	20	1.85	1.35	1	5
3214	Carpets and Rugs	13	2	3.83	4.70	1	20	1.50	0.50	1	2
32142	Wool	18	2	3.83	4.70	1	20	1.50	0.50	1	2
322	Manufacture of Wearing Apparel except Footwear	10	1	1.60	2.06	—	6	1.00	—	1	1
324	Manufacture of Footwear except Vulcanised or Moulded Rubber or Plastic Footwear	19	12	2.26	1.25	1	7	1.83	1.06	1	5
3241	Leather Footwear	19	12	2.26	1.25	1	7	1.85	1.06	1	5
325	Ginning, Pressing and Baling of Fibres	—	1	—	—	—	—	2.00	—	2	2
33	Manufacture of Wood and Wood Products including Furniture	126	44	2.50	1.32	1	7	2.56	1.34	1	6
331	Manufacture of Wood and Cork Products Except Furniture	73	28	2.72	1.35	1	7	3.14	1.27	1	6
3311	Saw and Planing Mills	47	22	3.08	1.18	1	7	3.13	1.18	1	6
3313	Wood Articles	15	4	2.60	1.58	1	6	3.00	1.87	1	6

Contd.

TABLE 1 (Contd.)
Rural Industry Male Workers

	Industry Major Group	Total Units		Total Male Workers							
				Irrigated				Rainfed			
		Irrigated	Rainfed	Mean	S.D	Minimum Value	Maximum Value	Mean	S.D	Minimum Value	Maximum Value
		(1)	(2)	(3)	(4)	(5)	(6)	(7)	(8)	(9)	(10)
332	Manufacture of Furniture and Fixtures Except Primarily of Metal	53	16	2.20	1.22	1	6	1.56	0.70	1	3
3321	Wooden Furniture	52	16	2.21	1.23	1	6	1.56	0.70	1	3
35	Manufacture of Chemicals and Chemical, Petroleum, Coal, Rubber and Plastic Products	6	—	3.16	2.11	1	6	—	—	—	—
352	Manufacture of other Chemical Products	4	—	4.25	1.78	2	6	—	—	—	—
355	Manufacture of Rubber Products	1	—	1.00	—	1	1	—	—	—	—
356	Manufacture of Plastic Products	1	—	1.00	—	1	1	—	—	—	—
36	Manufacture of Non-Metallic Mineral Products Except Petroleum and Coal	33	21	10.42	21.11	1	107	8.09	15.34	1	76
361	Manufacture of Pottery, China and Earthenware	11	2	2.27	0.56	1	5	1.50	0.50	1	2
369	Manufacture of Other Non-Metallic Mineral Products	22	19	14.50	24.86	1	107	8.78	15.97	2	76
3691	Manufacture of Bricks, Tiles and Other Structural Clay Products	18	13	17.27	26.70	2	107	11.15	18.84	2	76

Contd.

TABLE 1 (Contd.)

Rural Industry Male Workers

	Industry Major Group	Total Units		Total Male Workers							
				Irrigated				Rainfed			
		Irrigated	Rainfed	Mean	S.D	Minimum Value	Maximum Value	Mean	S.D	Minimum Value	Maxi mum Value
		(1)	(2)	(3)	(4)	(5)	(6)	(7)	(8)	(9)	(10)
37	Basic Metal Industries	1	—	7.00	—	7	7	—	—	—	—
371	Iron and Steel Basic Industries	1	—	7.00	—	7	7	—	—	—	—
33	Manufacture of Fabricated Metal Product, Machinery and Equipment	73	17	2.42	1.37	1	7	2.23	1.86	1	9
380-381	Manufacture of Fabricated Metal Products Except Machinery and Equipment	61	12	2.22	1.31	1	7	1.91	0.86	1	4
3802	Hand and Edge Tools	43	5	2.02	0.93	1	5	1.20	0.40	1	2
3805	Structural Metal Products	10	5	3.10	2.17	1	7	2.60	0.80	2	4
382	Manufacture of Machinery Except Electrical	10	5	3.60	1.28	2	6	3.00	3.03	1	9
383	Manufacture of Electrical Machinery Apparatus, Appliances and Supplies	1	—	3.00	—	6	3	—	—	—	—
384	Manufacture of Transport Equipment	1	—	2.00	—	2	2	—	—	—	—
39	Other Manufacturing Industries and Handicrafts	6	6	2.00	2.31	—	7	4.33	2.92	1	10
391	Handicrafts	3	—	0.66	0.47	—	1	—	—	—	—
392	Manufacture of Sports and Athletic Goods	1	2	7.00	—	7	7	7.50	2.50	5	10
393-394	Other Manufacturing Industries	2	4	1.50	0.50	1	2	2.75	1.48	1	5

TABLE 2
Rural Industry Female Workers

	Industry Major Group	Total Units		Total Female Workers							
				Irrigated				Rainfed			
		Irrigated	Rainfed	Mean	S.D	Minimum Value	Maximum Value	Mean	S.D	Minimum Value	Maximum Value
		(1)	(2)	(3)	(4)	(5)	(6)	(7)	(8)	(9)	(10)
Total		426	174	0.23	0.82	—	6	0.20	2.27	—	30
37-38	Metal Industries	74	17	0.01	0.10	—	1	—	—	—	—
	Other Industries	352	157	0.27	0.89	—	6	0.22	2.39	—	30
3	Manufacturing	426	174	0.23	0.82	—	6	0.20	2.27	—	30
31	Manufacture of Food, Beverages and Tobacco	116	65	—	—	—	1	0.01	0.10	—	1
311-312	Food Manufacturing	103	64	—	—	—	—	0.01	.10	—	1
3115	Manufacture of Vegetable and Inedible Animal Oils and Fats	15	12	—	—	—	—	0.08	0.26	—	1
31152	Vegetable Oils Except Hydrogenated Oils and Cotton Seed Oils	15	11	—	—	—	—	0.09	0.28	—	1
3116	Grain Milling and Products thereof	76	42	—	—	—	—	—	—	—	—
31162	Wheat and Grain Milling except Rice	72	42	—	—	—	—	—	—	—	—
3117	Manufacture of Bakery Products	13	7	—	—	—	—	—	—	—	—
314	Tobacco Manufacturing	8	1	.12	.33	—	1	—	—	—	—

Contd.

TABLE 2 (Contd.)

Rural Industry Female Workers

	Industry Major Group	Total Units		Total Female Workers							
				Irrigated				Rainfed			
		Irrigated	Rainfed	Mean	S.D	Mini-mum Value	Maxi-mum Value	Mean	S.D	Mini-mum Value	Maxi mum Value
		(1)	(2)	(3)	(4)	(5)	(6)	(7)	(8)	(9)	(10)
32	Textile, Wearing Apparel and Leather Industries	65	21	1.12	1.55	—	6	.04	.20	—	1
320-321	Manufacture of Textiles	36	7	1.36	1.44	—	6	.14	.35	—	1
3214	Carpets and Rugs	18	2	1.94	1.65	—	6	0.50	0.50	—	1
32142	Wool	18	2	1.94	1.65	—	6	0.50	0.50	—	1
322	Manufacture of Wearing Apparel Except Footwear	10	1	2.40	2.01	—	6	—	—	—	—
324	Manufacture of Footwear Except Vulcanised or Moulded Rubber or Plastic Footwear	19	12	—	—	—	—	—	—	—	—
3241	Leather Footwear	19	12	—	—	—	—	—	—	—	—
325	Ginning, Pressing and Baling of Fibres	—	1	—	—	—	—	—	—	—	—
33	Manufacture of Wood and Wood Products Including Furniture	126	44	0.01	.17	—	2	—	—	—	—

Contd.

TABLE 2 (Contd.)

Rural Industry Female Workers

	Industry Major Group	Total Units		Total Female Workers							
				Irrigated				Rainfed			
		Irrigated	Rainfed	Mean	S.D	Minimum Value	Maximum Value	Mean	S.D	Minimum Value	Maximum Value
		(1)	(2)	(3)	(4)	(5)	(6)	(7)	(8)	(9)	(10)
331	Manufacture of Wood and Wood and Cork Products Except Furniture	73	23	—	—	—	—	—	—	—	—
3311	Saw and Planing Mills	47	22	—	—	—	—	—	—	—	—
3313	Wood Articles	15	4	—	—	—	—	—	—	—	—
332	Manufacture of Furniture and Fixtures Except Primarily of Metal	53	16	0.03	0.26	—	2	—	—	—	—
3321	Wooden Furniture	52	16	.03	.26	—	2	—	—	—	—
35	Manufacture of Chemicals and Chemical, Petroleum, Coal, Rubber and Plastic Products	6	—	—	—	—	—	—	—	—	—
352	Manufacture of Other Chemical Products	4	—	—	—	—	—	—	—	—	—
355	Manufacture of Rubber Products	1	—	—	—	—	—	—	—	—	—
356	Manufacture of Plastic Products N.E.C.	1	—	—	—	—	—	—	—	—	—

Contd.

TABLE 2 (Contd.)
Rural Industry Female Workers

	Industry Major Group	Total Units		Total Female Workers							
				Irrigated				Rainfed			
		Irrigated	Rainfed	Mean	S.D	Minimum Value	Maximum Value	Mean	S.D	Minimum Value	Maxi mum Value
		(1)	(2)	(3)	(4)	(5)	(6)	(7)	(8)	(9)	(10)
36	Manufacture of Non-Metallic Mineral Products Except Petroleum and Coal	33	21	0.48	1.16	—	6	1.57	6.37	30	—
361	Manufacture of Pottery, China and Earthenware	11	2	0.90	.79	—	2	1.50	.50	1	2
369	Manufacture of Other Non-Metallic Mineral Products	22	19	0.27	1.25	—	2	1.57	6.70	—	30
3691	Manufacture of Bricks, Tiles and Other Structural Clay Products	13	13	0.33	1.37	—	6	2.30	7.99	—	30
37	Basic Metal Industries	1	—	—	—	—	—	—	—	—	—
371	Iron and Steel Basic Industries	1	—	—	—	—	—	—	—	—	—
38	Manufacture of Fabricated Metal Product, Machinery and Equipment	73	17	0.01	.10	—	1	—	—	—	—
380-381	Manufacture of Fabricated Metal Products Except Machinery and Equipment	61	12	0.01	.10	—	1	—	—	—	—
3802	Hand and Edge Tools	43	5	0.02	.14	—	1	—	—	—	—
3805	Structural Metal Products	10	5	—	—	—	—	—	—	—	—
382	Manufacture of Machinery Except										

Contd.

TABLE 2 (Contd.)
Rural Industry Female Workers

	Industry Major Group	Total Units		Total Workers							
				Irrigated				Rainfed			
		Irrigated	Rainfed	Mean	S.D	Minimum Value	Maximum Value	Mean	S.D	Minimum Value	Maximum Value
		(1)	(2)	(3)	(4)	(5)	(6)	(7)	(8)	(9)	(10)
	Electrical	10	5	—	—	—	—	—	—	—	—
383	Manufacture of Electrical Machinery Apparatus, Appliances and Supplies	1	—	—	—	—	—	—	—	—	—
384	Manufacture of Transport Equipment	1	—	—	—	—	—	—	—	—	—
39	Other Manufacturing Industries and Handicrafts	6	6	1.00	1.00	—	2	—	—	—	—
391	Handicrafts	3	—	2.00	—	2	2	—	—	—	—
392	Manufacture of Sports and Athletic Goods	1	2	—	—	—	—	—	—	—	—
393-394	Other Manufacturing Industries	2	4	—	—	—	—	—	—	—	—

TABLE 3

Rural Industrial Units by Size of Fixed Assets

	Industry Major Group	Number of Units		Value of Fixed Assets (Rs.)		Value of Fixed Assets (Rs.)			
						Per Unit		Per Worker	
		Irrigated	Rainfed	Irrigated	Rainfed	Irrigated	Rainfed	Irrigated	Rainfed
		(1)	(2)	(3)	(4)	(5)	(6)	(7)	(8)
Total		426	174	12811604	6714520	30074.18	38589.19	8501.39	11759.22
37-38	Metal Industries	74	17	1381210	692500	18665.00	40741.17	7466.00	18226.31
	Other Industries	352	157	11430394	6021920	32472.71	38356.17	8646.28	11298.16
3	Manufacturing	426	174	12811604	6714520	30074.18	38589.19	8501.39	11759.22
31	Manufacture of Food, Beverages and Tobacco	116	65	5908880	3396570	30933.32	52254.92	16144.48	22345.85
311-312	Food Manufacturing	108	64	5884200	3328570	54483.33	52008.90	16812.00	22490.33
3115	Manufacture of Vegetable and Inedible Animal Oils and Fats	15	12	784900	555900	52325.55	79658.33	16352.08	39825.16
31152	Vegetable Oils Except Hydrogenated	15	11	784900	652900	52626.66	59354.54	16352.08	36272.22
	Oils and Cotton Seed Oils								
3116	Grain Milling and Products Thereof	76	42	4065250	1961120	51742.36	46693.33	18478.40	22035.05
31162	Wheat and Grain Milling Except Rice	72	42	3725450	1961120	51742.36	46693.33	18084.70	22035.05
3117	Manufacture of Bakery Products	13	7	382450	127350	29419.23	18192.85	6168.54	4391.37

Contd.

TABLE 3 (Contd.)

Rural Industrial Units by Size of Fixed Assets

	Industry Major Group	Number of Units		Value of Fixed Assets (Rs.)		Value of Fixed Assets (Rs.) Per Unit		Value of Fixed Assets (Rs.) Per Worker	
		Irrigated	Rainfed	Irrigated	Rainfed	Irrigated	Rainfed	Irrigated	Rainfed
		(1)	(2)	(3)	(4)	(5)	(6)	(7)	(8)
314	Tobacco Manufacturing	8	1	24680	68000	8085.00	68000.00	1542.50	17000.00
32	Textile, Wearing Apparel and Leather Industries	65	21	1354894	199250	20344.52	9488.09	5612.96	5108.97
320-321	Manufacture of Textiles	36	7	756230	114500	21006.38	16357.14	4786.26	8178.57
3214	Carpets and Rugs	18	2	444880	12750	24715.55	6375.00	4277.69	3187.50
32142	Wool	18	2	444830	12750	24715.55	6375.00	4277.69	3187.50
322	Manufacture of Wearing Apparel Except Footwear	10	1	476254	29200	47625.40	29200.00	11906.35	29200.00
324	Manufacture of Footwear Except Vulcanised or Moulded Rubber or Plastic Footwear	19	12	122410	51250	6442.63	4270.83	2846.74	2329.54
3241	Leather Footwear	19	12	122410	51250	6442.63	4270.83	2846.74	2329.54
325	Ginning, Pressing and Baling of Fibres	—	1	—	4300	—	4300.00	—	2150.00
33	Manufacture of Wood and Wood Products including Furniture	126	44	3157360	1701700	25058.41	33675.00	9928.80	15059.25
331	Manufacture of Wood and Wood and Cork Products Except Furniture	73	28	2615710	1543850	35831.64	55137.50	13144.27	17543.75

Contd.

TABLE 3 Contd.)

Rural Industrial Units by Size of Fixed Assets

	Industry Major Group	Number of Units		Value of Fixed Assets (Rs.)		Value of Fixed Assets (Rs.)			
						Per Unit		Per Worker	
		Irrigated	Rainfed	Irrigated	Rainfed	Irrigated	Rainfed	Irrigated	Rainfed
		(1)	(2)	(3)	(4)	(5)	(6)	(7)	(8)
3311	Saw and Planing Mills	47	22	2061150	138450	43854.25	62925.00	14214.82	20063.04
3313	Wood Articles	15	4	331200	119500	22080.00	29875.00	8492.30	9958.33
332	Manufacture of Furniture and Fixtures Except Primarily of Metal	53	16	541650	157350	10219.81	9865.62	4551.68	6314.00
3321	Wooden Furniture	52	16	540850	157850	10400.96	9865.62	4622.64	6314.00
35	Manufacture of Chemicals and Chemical, Petroleum, Coal, Rubber and Plastic Products	6	—	208400	—	34733.33	—	10968.42	—
352	Manufacture of Other Chemical Products	4	—	200800	—	50200.00	—	11811.76	—
355	Manufacture of Rubber Products	1	—	1500	—	1500.00	—	1500.00	
356	Manufacture of Plastic Products N.E.C.	1	—	6100	—	6100.00	—	61000.00	—
36	Manufacture of Non-Metallic Mineral Products Except Petroleum and Coal	33	21	773000	667300	23575.75	31776.19	2161.11	3287.19

Contd.

TABLE 3 Contd.)

Rural Industrial Units by Size of Fixed Assets

	Industry Major Group	Number of Units		Value of Fixed Assets (Rs.)		Value of Fixed Assets (Rs.) Per Unit		Value of Fixed Assets (Rs.) Per Worker	
		Irrigated	Rainfed	Irrigated	Rainfed	Irrigated	Rainfed	Irrigated	Rainfed
		(1)	(2)	(3)	(4)	(5)	(6)	(7)	(8)
361	Manufacture of Pottery, China and Earthenware	11	2	35450	15700	3222.72	7850.00	1012.85	2616.66
369	Manufacture of Other Non-Metallic Mineral Products	22	19	742550	651600	33752.27	34294.73	2284.76	3307.61
3691	Manufacture of Bricks, Tiles and Other Structural Clay Products	18	13	660150	565100	38875.00	43469.23	2082.49	3229.14
37	Basic Metal Industries	1	—	220000	—	220000.00	—	31428.57	
371	Iron and Steel Basic Industries	1	—	220000	—	220000.00	—	31428.57	
38	Manufacture of Fabricated Metal Product, Machinery and Equipment	73	17	1161210	692600	15900.98	40741.17	6523.65	18226.31
380-381	Manufacture of Fabricated Metal Products Except Machinery and Equipment	61	12	496110	135800	8132.95	11316.66	3621.24	5904.34
3802	Hand and Edge Tools	43	5	308410	62200	7172.62	12440.00	3504.65	10366.66
3805	Structural Metal Products	10	5	117300	61900	11730.00	12380.00	3783.87	4761.53

Contd.

TABLE 3 Contd.)

Rural Industrial Units by Size of Fixed Assets

	Industry Major Group	Number of Units		Value of Fixed Assets (Rs.)		Value of Fixed Assets (Rs.)			
						Per Unit		Per Worker	
		Irrigated	Rainfed	Irrigated	Rainfed	Irrigated	Rainfed	Irrigated	Rainfed
		(1)	(2)	(3)	(4)	(5)	(6)	(7)	(8)
382	Manufacture of machinery Except Electrical	10	5	653100	356800	65310.00	111360.00	18141.66	37120.00
383	Manufacture of Electrical Machinery Apparatus, Appliances and Supplies	1	—	10800	—	10800.00	—	3600.00	—
384	Manufacture of Transport Equipment	1	—	1200	—	1200.00	—	600.00	—
39	Other Manufacturing Industries and Handicrafts	6	6	22860	57100	3610.00	9516.66	1270.00	2196.15
391	Handicrafts	3	—	400	—	133.33	—	50.00	—
392	Manufacture of Sports and Athletic Goods	1	2	460	29100	460.00	14550.00	65.71	1940.00
393-394	Other Manufacturing Industries	2	4	22000	28000	11000.00	7000.00	7333.33	2545.45

TABLE 4 (Contd.)

Growth of Rural Industrial Firms

Industry Major Group		Number of Units	Firms Reporting Sale Increase Over Last Three Years					
			Irrigated					
		Irrigated	Upto 10 %	11-20%	21-30%	31-40%	41-50%	Over 50%
		(1)	(2)	(3)	(4)	(5)	(6)	(7)
Total		426	413	9	4	—	—	—
37-38	Metal Industries	74	73	1	—	—	—	—
Other Industries		352	340	8	4	—	—	—
3	Manufacturing	426	413	9	4	—	—	—
31	Manufacture of Food, Beverages and Tobacco	116	114	2	—	—	—	—
311-312	Food Manufacturing	108	106	2	—	—	—	—
3115	Manufacture of Vegetable and Inedible Animal Oils and Fats	15	15	—	—	—	—	—
31152	Vegetable Oils except Hydrogenated Oils and Cotton Seed Oils	15	15	—	—	—	—	—
3116	Grain Milling and Products thereof	76	75	1	—	—	—	—
31162	Wheat and Grain Milling Except Rice	72	71	1	—	—	—	—
3117	Manufacture of Bakery Products	13	13	—	—	—	—	—
314	Tobacco Manufacturing	8	8	—	—	—	—	—
32	Textile, Wearing Apparel and Leather Industries	65	61	3	1	—	—	—
320-321	Manufacture of Textiles	36	34	1	1	—	—	—
3214	Carpets and Rugs	18	18	—	—	—	—	—
32142	Wool	18	18	—	—	—	—	—

Contd.

TABLE 4 (Contd.)

Growth of Rural Industrial Firms

Industry Major Group		Number of Units	Firms Reporting Sale Increase Over Last Three Years					
			Irrigated					
		Irrigated	Upto 10 %	11-20%	21-30%	31-40%	41-50%	Over 50%
		(1)	(2)	(3)	(4)	(5)	(6)	(7)
322	Manufacture of Wearing Apparel Except Footwear	10	9	1	—	—	—	—
324	Manufacture of Footwear Except Vulcanised or Moulded Rubber or Plastic Footwear	19	18	1	—	—	—	—
3241	Leather Footwear	19	18	1	—	—	—	—
33	Manufacture of Wood and Wood Products Including Furniture	126	121	3	2	—	—	—
331	Manufacture of Wood and Wood and Cork Products except Furniture	73	70	2	1	—	—	—
3311	Saw and Planing Mills	47	46	1	—	—	—	—
3313	Wood Articles	15	13	1	1	—	—	—
332	Manufacture of Furniture and Fixtures Except Primarily of Metal	53	51	1	1	—	—	—
3321	Wooden Furniture	52	50	1	1	—	—	—
35	Manufacture of Chemicals and Chemical, Petroleum, Coal, Rubber and Plastic Products	6	5	—	1	—	—	—
352	Manufacture of other Chemical Products	4	3	—	1	—	—	—

Contd.

TABLE 4 (Contd.)

Growth of Rural Industrial Firms

Industry Major Group		Number of Units	Firms Reporting Sale Increase Over Last Three Years					
			Irrigated					
		Irrigated	Upto 10 %	11-20%	21-30%	31-40%	41-50%	Over 50%
		(1)	(2)	(3)	(4)	(5)	(6)	(7)
355	Manufacture of Rubber Products	1	1	—	—	—	—	—
356	Manufacture of Plastic Products N.E.C.	1	1	—	—	—	—	—
36	Manufacture of Non-Metallic Mineral Products Except Petroleum and Coal	33	33	—	—	—	—	—
361	Manufacture of Pottery, China and Earthenware	11	11	—	—	—	—	—
369	Manufacture of Other Non-Metallic Mineral Products	22	22	—	—	—	—	—
3691	Manufacture of Bricks, Tiles and Other Structural Clay Products	18	18	—	—	—	—	—
37	Basic Metal Industries	1	1	—	—	—	—	—
371	Iron and Steel Basic Industries	1	1	—	—	—	—	—
33	Manufacture of Fabricated Metal Product, Machinery and Equipment	73	72	1	—	—	—	—
380-381	Manufacture of Fabricated Metal Products Except Machinery and Equipment	61	60	1	—	—	—	—
3802	Hand and Edge Tools	43	42	1	—	—	—	—
3805	Structural Metal Products	10	10	—	—	—	—	—

Contd.

TABLE 4 (Contd.)

Growth of Rural Industrial Firms

Industry Major Group		Number of Units	Firms Reporting Sale Increase Over Last Three Years					
			Irrigated					
		Irrigated	Upto 10 %	11-20%	21-30%	31-40%	41-50%	Over 50%
		(1)	(2)	(3)	(4)	(5)	(6)	(7)
382	Manufacture of Machinery except Electrical	10	10	—	—	—	—	—
383	Manufacture of Electrical Machinery Apparatus, Appliances and Supplies	1	1	—	—	—	—	—
384	Manufacture of Transport Equipment	1	1	—	—	—	—	—
39	Other Manufacturing Industries and Handicrafts	6	6	—	—	—	—	—
391	Handicrafts	3	3	—	—	—	—	—
392	Manufacture of Sports and Athletic Goods	1	1	—	—	—	—	—
393-394	Other Manufacturing Industries	2	2	—	—	—	—	—

TABLE 4 (Contd.)

Growth of Rural Industrial Firms

Industry Major Group		Number of Units	Firms Reporting Sale Increase Over Last Three Years					
			Irrigated					
		Irrigated	Upto 10 %	11-20%	21-30%	31-40%	41-50%	Over 50%
		(8)	(9)	(10)	(11)	(12)	(13)	(14)
Total		174	158	13	1	—	2	—
37-38	Metal Industries	17	15	2	—	—	—	—
	Other Industries	157	143	11	1	—	2	—
3	Manufacturing	174	158	13	1	—	2	—
31	Manufacture of Food, Beverages and Tobacco	65	62	2	—	—	1	—
311-312	Food Manufacturing	64	61	2	—	—	1	—
3115	Manufacture of Vegetable and Inedible Animal Oils and Fats	12	11	1	—	—	—	—
31152	Vegetable Oils Except Hydrogenated Oils and Cotton Seed Oils	11	10	1	—	—	—	—
3116	Grain Milling and Products Thereof	42	40	1	—	—	1	—
31162	Wheat and Grain Milling Except Rice	42	40	1	—	—	1	—
3117	Manufacture of Bakery Products	7	7	—	—	—	—	—
314	Tobacco Manufacturing	1	1	—	—	—	—	—
32	Textile, Wearing Apparel and Leather Industries	21	19	2	—	—	—	—
320-321	Manufacture of Textiles	7	7	—	—	—	—	—
3214	Carpets and Rugs	2	2	—	—	—	—	—

Contd.

TABLE 4 (Contd.)

Growth of Rural Industrial Firms

Industry Major Group		Number of Units	Firms Reporting Sale Increase Over Last Three Years					
			Irrigated					
		Irrigated	Upto 10 %	11-20%	21-30%	31-40%	41-50%	Over 50%
		(8)	(9)	(10)	(11)	(12)	(13)	(14)
32142	Wool	2	2	—	—	—	—	—
322	Manufacture of Wearing Apparel Except Footwear	1	1	—	—	—	—	—
324	Manufacture of Footwear Except Vulcanised or Moulded Rubber or Plastic Footwear	12	10	2	—	—	—	—
3241	Leather Footwear	12	10	2	—	—	—	—
325	Ginning, Pressing and Baling of Fibres	1	1	—	—	—	—	—
33	Manufacture of Wood and Wood Products Including Furniture	44	40	3	—	—	1	—
331	Manufacture of Wood and Wood and Cork Products Except Furniture	28	25	2	—	—	1	—
3311	Saw and Planing Mills	22	20	1	—	—	1	—
3313	Wood Articles	4	3	1	—	—	—	—
332	Manufacture of Furniture and Fixtures Except Primarily of Metal	16	— 15	1	—	—	—	—
3321	Wooden Furniture	16	15	1	—	—	—	—
36	Manufacture of Non-Metallic Mineral Products Except Petroleum and Coal	21	16	4	1	—	—	—

Contd.

TABLE 4 (Contd.)

Growth of Rural Industrial Firms

Industry Major Group		Number of Units	Firms Reporting Sale Increase Over Last Three Years					
			Irrigated					
		Irrigated	Upto 10 %	11-20%	21-30%	31-40%	41-50%	Over 50%
		(8)	(9)	(10)	(11)	(12)	(13)	(14)
361	Manufacture of Pottery, China and Earthenware	2	2	—	—	—	—	—
369	Manufacture of Other Non-Metallic Mineral Products	19	14	4	1	—	—	—
3691	Manufacture of Bricks, Tiles and Other Structural Clay Products	13	9	3	1	—	—	—
33	Manufacture of Fabricated Metal Product, Machinery and Equipment	17	15	2	—	—	—	—
380-381	Manufacture of Fabricated Metal Products Except Machinery and Equipment	12	11	1	—	—	—	—
3802	Hand and Edge Tools	5	5	—	—	—	—	
3805	Structural Metal Products	5	5	—	—	—	—	—
382	Manufacture of Machinery Except Electrical	5	4	1	—	—	—	—
39	Other Manufacturing Industries and Handicrafts	6	6	—	—	—	—	—
392	Manufacture of Sports and Athletic Goods	2	2	—	—	—	—	—
393-394	Other Manufacturing Industries	4	4	—	—	—	—	—

TABLE 5

Growth Constraints of Rural Industrial Firms

Industry Major Group		Number of Units		Capital Shortage		Lack of Technical Know-How		Skills Shortage		Limited Marketing Size		Technology	
		Irri-gated	Rain-fed	Irri-gated	Rain-fed	Irri-gated	Rain-fed	Irri-gated	Rain-fed	Irri-gated	Rain-fed	Irri-gated	Rain-fed
		(1)	(2)	(3)	(4)	(5)	(6)	(7)	(8)	(9)	(10)	(11)	(12)
Total		426	174	300	124	12	11	27	13	145	60	27	7
37-38	Metal Industries	74	17	56	10	—	2	2	4	29	8	3	—
	Other Industries	352	157	244	114	12	5	23	5	116	52	24	7
3	Manufacturing	426	174	300	124	12	11	27	13	145	60	27	7
31	Manufacture of Food, Beverages and Tobacco	116	65	69	48	4	4	6	2	43	19	6	2
311-312	Food Manufacturing	108	64	65	48	4	4	6	2	39	13	6	2
3115	Manufacture of Vegetable and Inedible Animal Oils and Fats	15	12	12	10	—	1	2	1	4	4	—	—
31152	Vegetable Oils Except Hydrogenated Oils and Cotton Seed Oils	15	11	12	9	—	1	2	1	4	4	—	—
3116	Grain Milling and Products thereof	76	42	40	29	3	2	4	1	26	13	4	1
31162	Wheat and Grain Milling Except Rice	72	42	38	29	2	2	3	1	23	13	4	1

Contd.

TABLE 5 (Contd.)

Growth Constraints of Rural Industrial Firms

Code	Industry Major Group	Number of Units		Capital Shortage		Lack of Technical Know-How		Skills Shortage		Limited Marketing Size		Technology	
		Irri-gated	Rain-fed	Irri-gated	Rain-fed	Irri-gated	Rain-fed	Irri-gated	Rain-fed	Irri-gated	Rain-fed	Irri-gated	Rain-fed
		(1)	(2)	(3)	(4)	(5)	(6)	(7)	(8)	(9)	(10)	(11)	(12)
3117	Manufacture of Bakery Products	13	7	9	6	1	1	2	—	5	—	2	1
314	Tobacco Manufacturing	8	1	4	—	—	—	—	—	4	1	—	—
32	Textile, Wearing Apparel and Leather Industries	65	21	49	17	1	2	2	1	18	5	4	3
320-321	Manufacture of Textiles	36	7	26	6	1	—	1	—	11	2	2	2
3214	Carpets and Rugs	13	2	14	2	1	—	—	—	8	1	—	—
32142	Wool	13	2	14	2	1	—	—	—	8	1	—	—
322	Manufacture of Wearing Apparel Except Footwear	10	1	9	1	—	—	—	—	2	—	2	—
324	Manufacture of Footwear Except Vulcanised or Moulded Rubber or Plastic Footwear	19	12	14	9	—	2	1	1	5	3	—	1
3241	Leather Footwear	19	12	14	9	—	2	1	1	5	3	—	1
325	Ginning, Pressing a nd Baling of Fibres	—	1	—	1	—	—	—	—	—	—	—	—

Contd.

TABLE 5 (Contd.)

Growth Constraints of Rural Industrial Firms

Industry Major Group		Number of Units		Capital Shortage		Lack of Technical Know-How		Skills Shortage		Limited Marketing Size		Technology	
		Irri-gated	Rain-fed	Irri-gated	Rain-fed	Irri-gated	Rain-fed	Irri-gated	Rain-fed	Irri-gated	Rain-fed	Irri-gated	Rain-fed
		(1)	(2)	(3)	(4)	(5)	(6)	(7)	(8)	(9)	(10)	(11)	(12)
33	Manufacture of Wood and Wood Products Including Furniture	126	44	91	33	7	2	10	2	43	20	11	2
331	Manufacture of Wood and Wood and Cork Products Except Furniture	73	28	47	21	2	1	6	1	24	10	7	1
3311	Saw and Planing Mills	47	22	33	16	—	1	6	1	10	8	5	1
3313	Wood Articles	15	4	13	4	2	—	1	—	9	2	2	—
332	Manufacture of Furniture and Fixtures Except Primarily of Metal	53	16	44	12	5	1	4	1	19	10	4	1
3321	Wooden Furniture	52	16	44	12	5	1	4	1	19	10	4	1
35	Manufacture of Chemicals and Chemical, Petroleum, Coal, Rubber and Plastic Products	6	—	5	—	—	—	—	—	2	—	—	—
352	Manufacture of Other Chemical Products												

Contd.

TABLE 5 (Contd.)

Growth Constraints of Rural Industrial Firms

	Industry Major Group	Number of Units		Capital Shortage		Lack of Technical Know-How		Skills Shortage		Limited Marketing Size		Technology	
		Irri-gated	Rain-fed	Irri-gated	Rain-fed	Irri-gated	Rain-fed	Irri-gated	Rain-fed	Irri-gated	Rain-fed	Irri-gated	Rain-fed
		(1)	(2)	(3)	(4)	(5)	(6)	(7)	(8)	(9)	(10)	(11)	(12)
355	Manufacture of Rubber	4	—	3	—	—	—	—	—	1	—	—	—
	Products	1	—	1	—	—	—	—	—	1	—	—	—
356	Manufacture of Plastic Products N.E.C.	1	—	1	—	—	—	—	—	—	—	—	—
36	Manufacture of Non-Metallic Mineral Products Except Petroleum and Coal	33	21	24	11	—	1	4	4	8	7	2	—
361	Manufacture of Pottery, China and Earthenware	11	2	7	—	—	—	—	—	3	1	2	—
369	Manufacture of Other Non-MetallicMineral Products	22	19	17	11	—	1	4	4	5	6	—	—
3691	Manufacture of Bricks, Tiles and Other Structural Clay Products	18	13	14	8	—	—	4	3	2	4	—	—
37	Basic Metal Industries	1	—	1	—	—	—		—	—	—	1	—
371	Iron and Steel Basic Industries	1	—	1	—	—	—	—	—	—	—	1	—

Contd.

TABLE 5 (Contd.)

Growth Constraints of Rural Industrial Firms

	Industry Major Group	Number of Units		Capital Shortage		Lack of Technical Know-How		Skills Shortage		Limited Marketing Size		Technology	
		Irri-gated	Rain-fed	Irri-gated	Rain-fed	Irri-gated	Rain-fed	Irri-gated	Rain-fed	Irri-gated	Rain-fed	Irri-gated	Rain-fed
		(1)	(2)	(3)	(4)	(5)	(6)	(7)	(8)	(9)	(10)	(11)	(12)
38	Manufacture of Fabricated Metal Product, Machinery and Equipment	73	17	55	10	—	2	2	4	29	8	2	—
380-381	Manufacture of Fabricated Metal Products Except Machinery and Equipment	61	12	43	7	—	1	—	3	22	5	2	—
3802	Hand and Edge Tools	43	5	28	1	—	—	—	—	17	—	2	—
3805	Structural Metal Products	10	5	9	4	—	—	—	3	5	4	—	—
382	Manufacture of Machinery Except Electrical	10	5	10	3	—	1	1	1	6	3	–	—
383	Manufacture of Electrical Machinery Apparatus, Appliances and Supplies	1	—	1	—	—	—	—	—	—	—	—	—
384	Manufacture of Transport Equipment	1	—	1	—	—	—	1	—	1	—	—	—
39	Other Manufacturing Industries and	6	6	6	5	—	—	1	—	2	1	1	—

Contd.

TABLE 5 (Contd.)

Growth Constraints of Rural Industrial Firms

Industry Major Group		Number of Units		Capital Shortage		Lack of Technical Know-How		Skills Shortage		Limited Marketing Size		Technology	
		Irri-gated	Rain-fed	Irri-gated	Rain-fed	Irri-gated	Rain-fed	Irri-gated	Rain-fed	Irri-gated	Rain-fed	Irri-gated	Rain-fed
		(1)	(2)	(3)	(4)	(5)	(6)	(7)	(8)	(9)	(10)	(11)	(12)
	Handicrafts												
391	Handicrafts	3	—	3	—	—	—	—	—	—	—	1	—
392	Manufacture of Sports and Athletic Goods	1	2	1	2	—	—	—	—	—	—	—	—
393-394	Other Manufacturing Industries	2	4	2	3	—	—	1	—	2	1	—	—

Contd.

TABLE 5

Growth Constraints of Rural Industrial Firms

Industry Major Group		Lack of Marketing facilities		Management Limitations		Lack of Raw Materials		Lack of Specialised Services		Lack of Energy	
		Irrigated	Rainfed	Irrigated	Rainfed	Irrigated	Rainfed	Irrigated	Rainfed	Irrigated	Rainfed
		(13)	(14)	(15)	(16)	(17)	(18)	(19)	(20)	(21)	(22)
Total		41	20	—	1	50	24	6	1	20	28
37-38	Metal Industries	8	2	—	—	12	4	2	—	3	4
	Other Industries	33	16	—	1	38	20	6	1	17	24
3	Manufacturing	41	20	—	1	50	24	6	1	20	28
31	Manufacture of Food, Beverages and Tobacco	11	4	—	—	12	4	2	—	9	12
311-312	Food Manufacturing	11	3	—	—	9	4	2	—	9	12
3115	Manufacture of Vegetable and Inedible Animal Oils and Fats	1	1	—	—	4	—	—	—	2	4
31152	Vegetable Oils Except Hydrogenated Oils and Cotton Seed Oils	1	1	—	—	4	—	—	—	2	4
3116	Grain Milling and Products Thereof	6	1	—	—	5	4	1	—	4	7
31162	Wheat and Grain Milling Except Rice	6	1	—	—	4	4	—	—	4	7

Contd.

TABLE 5 (Contd.)

Growth Constraints of Rural Industrial Firms

Industry Major Group		Lack of Marketing facilities		Management Limitations		Lack of Raw Materials		Lack of Specialised Services		Lack of Energy	
		Irrigated	Rainfed	Irrigated	Rainfed	Irrigated	Rainfed	Irrigated	Rainfed	Irrigated	Rainfed
		(13)	(14)	(15)	(16)	(17)	(18)	(19)	(20)	(21)	(22)
3117	Manufacture of Bakery Products	8	—	—	—	—	—	1	—	1	1
314	Tobacco Manufacturing	—	1	—	—	3	—	—	—	—	—
32	Textile, Wearing Apparel and Leather Industries	6	4	—	—	9	3	—	—	—	1
320-321	Manufacture of Textiles	2	2	—	—	6	2	—	—	1	—
3214	Carpets and Rugs	1	1	—	—	5	—	—	—	1	—
32142	Wool	1	1	—	—	5	—	—	—	1	—
322	Manufacture of Wearing Apparel Except Footwear	4	1	—	—	2	—	—	—	—	—
324	Manufacture of Footwear Except Vulcanised or Moulded- Rubber or Plastic Footwear	—	1	—	—	1	1	—	—	—	1
3241	Leather Footwear	—	1	—	—	1	1	—	—	—	1
325	Ginning, Pressing and Baling of Fibres	—	—	—	—	—	—	—	—	—	—

Contd.

TABLE 5 (Contd.)

Growth Constraints of Rural Industrial Firms

	Industry Major Group	Lack of Marketing facilities		Management Limita-tions		Lack of Raw Materials		Lack of Specialised Services		Lack of Energy	
		Irri-gated	Rain-fed	Irri-gated	Rain-fed	Irri-gated	Rain-fed	Irri-gated	Rain-fed	Irri-gated	Rain-fed
		(13)	(14)	(15)	(16)	(17)	(18)	(19)	(20)	(21)	(22)
33	Manufacture of Wood and Wood Products Including Furniture	11	5	—	1	12	8	2	—	5	6
331	Manufacture of Wood and Wood and Cork Products Except Furniture	5	3	—	—	5	7	2	—	2	6
3311	Saw and Planing Mills	3	1	—	—	3	7	2	—	2	5
3313	Wood Articles	2	1	—	—	2	—	—	—	—	1
332	Manufacture of Furniture and Fixtures Except Primarily of Metal	6	2	—	1	7	1	—	—	3	—
3321	Wooden Furniture	6	2	—	1	7	1	—	—	3	—
35	Manufacture of Chemicals and Chemical, Petroleum, Coal, Rubber and Plastic Products	—	—	—	—	2	—	—	—	1	—
352	Manufacture of Other Chemical Products	—	—	—	—	2	—	—	—	1	—

Contd.

TABLE 5 (Contd.)

Growth Constraints of Rural Industrial Firms

Industry Major Group		Lack of Marketing facilities		Management Limitations		Lack of Raw Materials		Lack of Specialised Services		Lack of Energy	
		Irrigated	Rainfed	Irrigated	Rainfed	Irrigated	Rainfed	Irrigated	Rainfed	Irrigated	Rainfed
		(13)	(14)	(15)	(16)	(17)	(18)	(19)	(20)	(21)	(22)
355	Manufacture of Rubber	—	—	—	—	—	—	—	—	—	—
	Products	—	—	—	—	—	—	—	—	—	—
356	Manufacture of Plastic Products N.E.C.	—	—	—	—	—	—	—	—	—	—
36	Manufacture of Non-Metallic Mineral Products Except Petroleum and Coal	4	4	—	—	3	5	4	1	1	5
361	Manufacture of Pottery, China and Earthenware	1	1	—	—	1	—	1	—	1	—
369	Manufacture of Other Non-Metallic Mineral Products	3	3	—	—	2	5	1	1	—	5
3691	Manufacture of Bricks, Tiles and Other Structural Clay Products	1	3	—	—	2	3	1	1	—	4
37	Basic Metal Industries	—	—	—	—	1	—	—	—	—	—
371	Iron and Steel Basic Industries	—	—	—	—	1	—	—	—	—	—

Contd.

TABLE 5 (Contd.)

Growth Constraints of Rural Industrial Firms

Industry Major Group		Lack of Marketing facilities		Management Limitations		Lack of Raw Materials		Lack of Specialised Services		Lack of Energy	
		Irrigated	Rainfed	Irrigated	Rainfed	Irrigated	Rainfed	Irrigated	Rainfed	Irrigated	Rainfed
		(13)	(14)	(15)	(16)	(17)	(18)	(19)	(20)	(21)	(22)
38	Manufacture of Fabricated Metal and Equipment	8	2	—	—	11	4	2	—	3	4
380-381	Manufacture of Fabricated Metal Products Except Machinery and Equipment	7	1	—	—	9	4	2	—	3	3
3802	Hand and Edge Tools	6	—	—	—	9	1	2	—	3	—
3805	Structural Metal Products	1	—	—	—	—	3	—	—	—	3
382	Manufacture of Machinery Except Electrical	1	1	—	—	1	—	—	—	—	1
383	Manufacture of Electrical Machinery Apparatus, Appliances and Supplies	—	—	—	—	—	—	—	—	—	—
384	Manufacture of Transport Equipment	—	—	—	—	1	—	—	—	—	—
39	Other Manufacturing Industries and Handicrafts	1	1	—	—	—	—	—	—	—	—
391	Handicrafts	1	—	—	—	—	—	—	—	—	—

Contd.

TABLE 5 (Contd.)

Growth Constraints of Rural Industrial Firms

Industry Major Group		Lack of Marketing facilities		Management Limitations		Lack of Raw Materials		Lack of Specialised Services		Lack of Energy	
		Irrigated	Rainfed	Irrigated	Rainfed	Irrigated	Rainfed	Irrigated	Rainfed	Irrigated	Rainfed
		(13)	(14)	(15)	(16)	(17)	(18)	(19)	(20)	(21)	(22)
392	Manufacture of Sports and Athletic Goods	—	1	—	—	—	—	—	—	—	—
393-394	Other Manufacturing Industries	—	—	—	—	—	—	—	—	—	—

TABLE 6

Rural Industrial Units Requiring Assistance for Skills Diffusion

Industry Major Group		Total Number of Units				Short Training Course			
		Irrigated		Rainfed		Irrigated		Rainfed	
		No	% Age	No	% Age	No	% Age	No.	% Age
		(1)	(2)	(3)	(4)	(5)	(6)	(7)	(8)
Total		426	100.00	174	100.00	122	28.64	41	23.56
37-38	Metal Industries	74	100.00	17	100.00	16	21.62	4	23.53
Other Industries		352	100.00	157	100.00	100	30.11	37	23.57
3	Manufacturing	426	100.00	174	100.00	122	28.64	41	23.56
31	Manufacture of Food, Beverages and Tobacco	116	100.00	65	100.00	39	33.62	19	29.23
311-312	Food Manufacturing	108	100.00	64	100.00	34	31.48	19	29.69
3115	Manufacture of Vegetable and Inedible Animal Oils and Fats	15	100.00	12	100.00	9	60.00	3	25.00
31152	Vegetable Oils Except Hydrogenated Oils and Cotton Seed Oils	15	100.00	11	100.00	9	60.00	3	27.27
3116	Grain Milling and Products thereof	76	100.00	42	100.00	20	26.32	16	38.10
31162	Wheat and Grain Milling except Rice	72	100.00	42	100.00	18	25.00	16	38.10
3117	Manufacture of Bakery Products	13	100.00	7	100.00	4	30.77	—	—
314	Tobacco Manufacturing	8	100.00	1	100.00	5	62.50	—	—
32	Textile, Wearing Apparel and Leather Industries	65	100.00	21	100.00	20	30.77	4	19.05
320-321	Manufacture of Textiles	36	100.00	7	100.00	13	36.11	1	14.29
3214	Carpets and Rugs	18	100.00	2	100.00	8	44.44	—	—

Contd.

TABLE 6 (Contd.)

Rural Industrial Units Requiring Assistance for Skills Diffusion

Industry Major Group		Total Number of Units				Short Training Course			
		Irrigated		Rainfed		Irrigated		Rainfed	
		No	% Age	No	% Age	No	% Age	No.	% Age
		(1)	(2)	(3)	(4)	(5)	(6)	(7)	(8)
32142	Wool	18	100.00	2	100.00	8	44.44	—	—
322	Manufacture of Wearing Apparel except Footwear	10	100.00	1	100.00	1	10.00	—	—
324	Manufacture of Footwear except Vulcanised or Moulded Rubber or Plastic Footwear	19	100.00	12	100.00	6	31.58	3	25.00
3241	Leather Footwear	19	100.00	12	100.00	6	31.58	3	25.00
325	Ginning, Pressing and Baling of Fibres	—	—	1	100.00	—	—	—	—
33	Manufacture of Wood and Wood Products Including Furniture	126	100.00	44	100.00	33	26.19	11	25.00
331	Manufacture of Wood and Wood and Cork Products Except Furniture	73	100.00	28	100.00	19	26.03	6	21.43
3311	Saw and Planing Mills	47	100.00	22	100.00	13	27.66	5	22.73
3313	Wood Articles	15	100.00	4	100.00	6	40.00	1	25.00
332	Manufacture of Furniture and Fixtures Except Primarily of Metal	53	100.00	16	100.00	14	26.42	5	31.25
3321	Wooden Furniture	52	100.00	16	100.00	14	26.92	5	31.25

Contd.

TABLE 6 (Contd.)

Rural Industrial Units Requiring Assistance for Skills Diffusion

Industry Major Group		Total Number of Units				Short Training Course			
		Irrigated		Rainfed		Irrigated		Rainfed	
		No	% Age	No	% Age	No	% Age	No.	% Age
		(1)	(2)	(3)	(4)	(5)	(6)	(7)	(8)
35	Manufacture of Chemicals and Chemical, Petroleum, Coal, Rubber and Plastic Products	6	100.00	—	—	1	16.67	—	—
352	Manufacture of Other Chemical Products	4	100.00	—	—	1	25.00	—	—
355	Manufacture of Rubber Products	1	100.00	—	—	—	—	—	—
356	Manufacture of Plastic Products N.E.C.	1	100.00	—	—	—	—	—	—
36	Manufacture of Non-Metallic Mineral Products Except Petroleum and Coal	33	100.00	21	100.00	12	36.36	3	14.25
361	Manufacture of Pottery, China and Earthenware	11	100.00	2	100.00	3	27.27	—	—
369	Manufacture of Other Non-Metallic Mineral Products	22	100.00	19	100.00	9	40.91	3	15.79
3691	Manufacture of Bricks, Tiles and Other Structural Clay Products	18	100.00	13	100.00	9	50.00	3	23.08
37	Basic Metal Industries	1	100.00	—	—	—	—	—	—
371	Iron and Steel Basic Industries	1	100.00	—	—	—	—	—	—

Contd.

TABLE 6 (Contd.)

Rural Industrial Units Requiring Assistance for Skills Diffusion

Industry Major Group		Total Number of Units				Short Training Course			
		Irrigated		Rainfed		Irrigated		Rainfed	
		No	% Age	No	% Age	No	% Age	No.	% Age
		(1)	(2)	(3)	(4)	(5)	(6)	(7)	(8)
38	Manufacture of Fabricated Metal Product, Machinery and Equipment	73	100.00	17	100.00	18	21.92	4	23.53
380-381	Manufacture of Fabricated Metal Products except Machinery and Equipment	61	100.00	12	100.00	13	21.31	3	25.00
3802	Hand and Edge Tools	43	100.00	5	100.00	10	23.26	—	—
3805	Structural Metal Products	10	100.00	5	100.00	2	20.00	3	60.00
382	Manufacture of Machinery Except Electrical	10	100.00	5	100.00	2	20.00	1	20.00
383	Manufacture of Electrical Machinery Apparatus, Appliances and Supplies	1	100.00	—	—	—	—	—	—
384	Manufacture of Transport Equipment	1	100.00	—	—	1	100	—	—
39	Other Manufacturing Industries and Handicrafts	6	100.00	6	100.00	1	16.67	—	—
391	Handicrafts	3	100.00	—	—	—	—	—	—
392	Manufacture of Sports and Athletic Goods	1	100.00	2	100.00	—	—	—	—
393-394	Other Manufacturing Industries	2	100.00	4	100.00	1	50.00	—	—

Contd.

TAbLE 6 (Contd.)

Rural Industrial Units Requiring Assistance for Skills Diffusion

Industry Major Group		Total Number of Units				Short Training Course			
		Irrigated		Rainfed		Irrigated		Rainfed	
		No	% Age	No	% Age	No	% Age	No.	% Age
		(9)	(10)	(11)	(12)	(13)	(14)	(15)	(16)
Total		110	25.82	34	19.54	180	42.25	90	51.72
37—38	Metal Industries	20	27.03	4	23.53	35	47.30	7	41.18
	Other Industries	90	25.57	30	19.11	145	41.19	83	52.87
3	Manufacturing	110	25.82	34	19.54	180	42.25	90	51.72
31	Manufacture of Food, Beverages and Tobacco	35	30.17	10	15.38	40	34.48	32	49.23
311-312	Food Manufacturing	34	31.48	10	15.63	40	37.04	31	48.44
3115	Manufacture of Vegetable and Inedible Animal Oils and Fats	6	40.00	1	8.33	7	46.67	9	75.00
31152	Vegetable Oils Except Hydrogenated Oils and Cotton Seed Oils	6	40.00	—	—	7	46.67	9	81.82
3116	Grain Milling and Products Thereof	20	26.32	5	11.90	28	36.84	18	42.86
31162	Wheat and Grain Milling Except Rice	19	26.39	5	11.90	28	38.89	18	42.86
3117	Manufacture of Bakery Products	6	46.15	3	42.86	4	30.77	4	57.14
314	Tobacco Manufacturing	1	12.50	—	—	—	—	1	100.00
32	Textile, Wearing Apparel and Leather Industries	11	16.92	4	19.05	28	43.08	11	52.38

Contd.

TABLE 6 (Contd.)

Rural Industrial Units Requiring Assistance for Skills Diffusion

Industry Major Group		Total Number of Units				Short Training Course			
		Irrigated		Rainfed		Irrigated		Rainfed	
		No	% Age	No	% Age	No	% Age	No.	% Age
		(9)	(10)	(11)	(12)	(13)	(14)	(15)	(16)
320-321	Manufacture of Textiles	7	19.44	2	28.57	15	41.67	2	28.57
3214	Carpets and Rugs	3	16.67	—	—	5	27.78	—	—
32142	Wool	3	16.67	—	—	5	27.78	—	—
322	Manufacture of Wearing Apparel Except Footwear	1	10.00	—	—	8	80.00	1	100.00
324	Manufacture of Footwear Except Vulcanised or Moulded Rubber or Plastic Footwear	3	15.75	2	16.67	5	26.32	7	58.33
3241	Leather Footwear	3	15.79	2	16.67	5	26.32	7	58.33
325	Ginning, Pressing and Baling of Fibres	—	—	—	—	—	—	1	100.00
33	Manufacture of Wood and Wood Products Including Furniture	34	26.98	10	22.73	61	48.41	28	63.64
331	Manufacture of Wood and Wood and Cork Products Except Furniture	17	23.25	4	14.29	41	56.16	18	64.29
3311	Saw and Planing Mills	14	29.79	3	13.64	25	53.19	17	77.27
3313	Wood Articles	3	20.00	1	25.00	5	33.33	1	25.00
332	Manufacture of Furniture and Fixtures Except Primarily of Metal	17	32.00	6	37.50	20	37.74	10	62.50

Contd.

TABLE 6 (Contd.)

Rural Industrial Units Requiring Assistance for Skills Diffusion

Industry Major Group		Total Number of Units				Short Training Course			
		Irrigated		Rainfed		Irrigated		Rainfed	
		No	% Age	No	% Age	No	% Age	No.	% Age
		(9)	(10)	(11)	(12)	(13)	(14)	(15)	(16)
3321	Wooden Furniture	17	32.69	6	37.50	20	38.46	10	62.50
35	Manufacture of Chemicals and Chemical, Petroleum, Coal, Rubber and Plastic Products	—	—	—	—	8	50.00	—	—
352	Manufacture of Other Chemical Products	—	—	—	—	2	50.00	—	—
355	Manufacture of Rubber Products	—	—	—	—	—	—	—	—
356	Manufacture of Plastic Products N.E.C.	—	—	—	—	1	100.00	—	—
36	Manufacture of Non-Metallic Mineral Products Except Petroleum and Coal	9	27.27	4	19.05	10	30.30	11	52.38
361	Manufacture of Pottery, China and Earthenware	1	9.09	1	50.00	4	36.36	1	50.00
369	Manufacture of Other Non-Metallic Mineral Products	8	36.36	3	15.79	6	27.27	10	52.63
3691	Manufacture of Bricks, Tiles and Other Structural Clay Products	7	38.89	3	23.38	6	33.33	7	53.85
37	Basic Metal Industries	—	—	—	—	1	100.00	—	—
371	Iron and Steel Basic Industries	—	—	—	—	1	100.00	—	—

Contd.

TABLE 6 (Contd.)

Rural Industrial Units Requiring Assistance for Skills Diffusion

Industry Major Group		Total Number of Units				Short Training Course			
		Irrigated		Rainfed		Irrigated		Rainfed	
		No	% Age	No	% Age	No	% Age	No.	% Age
		(9)	(10)	(11)	(12)	(13)	(14)	(15)	(16)
38	Manufacture of Fabricated Metal Product, Machinery and Equipment	20	27.40	4	23.53	34	46.58	7	41.18
380-381	Manufacture of Fabricated Metal Products except Machinery and Equipment	18	29.51	4	33.33	29	47.54	4	33.33
3802	Hand and Edge Tools	18	41.36	1	20.00	20	46.51	2	40.00
3805	Structural Metal Products	—	—	2	40.00	4	40.00	1	20.00
382	Manufacture of Machinery except Electrical	—	—	—	—	4	40.00	3	60.00
383	Manufacture of Electrical Machinery Apparatus, Appliances and Supplies	1	100.00	—	—	—	—	—	—
384	Manufacture of Transport Equipment	1	100.00	—	—	1	100.00	—	—
39	Other Manufacturing Industries and Handicrafts	1	16.67	2	33.33	8	50.00	1	16.67
391	Handicrafts	—	—	—	—	1	33.33	—	—
392	Manufacture of Sports and Athletic Goods	—	—	1	50.00	1	100.00	—	—
393-394	Other Manufacturing Industries	1	50.00	1	25.00	1	50.00	1	25.00

Annexe II
Tables from Project Urban Small Scale Industry Survey

TABLE 1

Urban, Informal Manufacturing
Proportion of Enterprises Stating Problems Faced in Starting/Entering Business of P Activity and by Type and Location of Units

All Manufacturing Activities

Type of Problems Faced	City								
	Karachi			Gujranwala					
	House Hold	Small Unit	Total	House Hold	Small Unit	Total	House Hold	Small Unit	Total
Lack of Capital	32.2%	33.6%	33.3%	51.5%	42.9%	45.5%	42.5%	37.7%	38.9%
	(19)	(72)	(91)	(35)	(70)	(105)	(54)	(142)	(136)
Lack of Raw	22.0%	20.1%	20.5%	14.7%	11.7%	12.6%	18.1%	16.4%	16.9%
Materials	(13)	(43)	(56)	(10)	(19)	(29)	(23)	(62)	(85)
Lack of Technical Skills	1.7%	8.4%	7.0%	7.4%	9.8%	9.1%	4.7%	9.0%	7.9%
	(1)	(18)	(19)	(5)	(16)	(21)	(6)	(34)	(40)
Lack of Equipment	1.7%	4.2%	3.7%	0.0%	1.2%	.9%	.8%	2.9%	2.4%
	(1)	(9)	(10)	(0)	(2)	(2)	(1)	(11)	(12)
Government Regulations	0.0%	1.4%	1.1%	0.0%	.6%	.4%	0.0%	1.1%	.8%
	(0)	(3)	(3)	(0)	(1)	(1)	(0)	(4)	(4)
Finding Suitable Premises	6.8%	17.8%	15.4%	10.3%	14.1%	13.0%	8.7%	15.2%	14.3%
	(4)	(38)	(42)	(7)	(23)	(30)	(11)	(61)	(72)
No Electricity	25.4%	1.4%	6.6%	0.0%	2.5%	1.7%	11.8%	1.9%	4.4%
	(15)	(3)	(18)	(0)	(4)	(4)	(15)	(7)	(22)

Contd.

TABLE 1 (Contd)

Urban, Informal Manufacturing
Proportion of Enterprises Stating Problems Faced in Starting/Entering Business of Activity and by Type and Location of Units

All Manufacturing Activities

Type of Problems Faced	City								
	Karachi			Gujranwala					
	House Hold	Small Unit	Total	House Hold	Small Unit	Total	House Hold	Small Unit	Total
No Water/Sewerage	5.1%	1.4%	2.2%	0.0%	1.2%	0.9%	2.4%	1.3%	1.6%
or GasConnections	(3)	(3)	(6)	(0)	(2)	(2)	(3)	(5)	(8)
Finding a Market for Goods	3.4%	11.7%	9.9%	14.7%	16.0%	15.6%	9.4%	13.5%	12.5%
	(2)	(25)	(27)	(10)	(26)	(36)	(12)	(51)	(63)
Other	1.7%	0.0%	0.4%	1.5%	0.0%	.4%	1.6%	0.0%	0.4%
	(1)	(0)	(1)	(1)	(0)	(1)	(2)	(0)	(2)

Number in Parenthesis.

Source: Project Urban Informal Manufacturing Survey, FBS 1990.

TABLE 2

Distribution of Urban, Informal Manufacturing Enterprises, Who Reported Change in Output in the Past 3 Years by Type of Manufacturing Activities and Location of Units—All Manufacturing Activities

Change in Demand for Output	City								
	Karachi			Gujranwala					
	House Hold	Small Unit	Total	House Hold	Small Unit	Total	House Hold	Small Unit	Total
A Substantive Increase	8.3%	6.4%	7.2%	0.0%	0.0%	0.0%	4.5%	2.7%	3.4%
	(3)	(3)	(6)	(0)	(0)	(0)	(3)	(3)	(6)
A Slight Increase	2.8%	29.8%	18.1%	20.0%	18.2%	18.8%	10.6%	23.0%	18.4%
	(1)	(14)	(15)	(6)	(12)	(18)	(7)	(26)	(33)
A Slight Decrease	80.6%	51.1%	63.9%	6.7%	3.0%	4.2%	47.0%	23.0%	31.8%
	(29)	(24)	(53)	(2)	(2)	(4)	(31)	(26)	(57)
A Substantive Decrease	2.8%	0.0%	1.2%	0.0%	12.1%	8.3%	1.5%	7.1%	5.0%
	(1)	(0)	(1)	(0)	(8)	(8)	(1)	(8)	(9)
No Change in Demand	2.8%	10.6%	7.2%	73.3%	66.7%	68.8%	34.8%	43.4%	40.2%
	(1)	(5)	(6)	(22)	(44)	(66)	(23)	(49)	(72)
Not Applicable	2.8%	2.1%	2.4%	0.0%	0.0%	0.0%	1.5%	0.9%	1.1%
	(1)	(1)	(2)	(0)	(0)	(0)	(1)	(1)	(2)
Total	(36)	(47)	(83)	(30)	(66)	(96)	(66)	(113)	(179)
	43.4%	56.6%	100.0%	31.3%	68.8%	100.0%	36.9%	63.1%	100.1%

Number in Parenthesis.
Source: Project Urban Informal Manufacturing Survey, FBS 1990.

TABLE 3

Urban, Informal Manufacturing
Distribution of Enterprises by Problems Being Faced at Present and By Type and Location of Units
All Manufacturing Activities

Problems Being Faced at Present	City								
	Karachi			Gujranwala					
	House Holds	Small Units	Total	House Holds	Small Units	Total	House Holds	Small Units	Total
	1.5%	.4%	.8%	0.0%	0.0%	0.0%	.7%	.2%	.4%
	(2)	(1)	(3)	(0)	(0)	(0)	(2)	(1)	(3)
Lack of Supervision	.8%	0.0%	.3%	0.0%	0.0%	0.0%	.4%	0.0%	.1%
	(1)	(0)	(1)	(0)	(0)	(0)	(1)	(0)	(1)
Lack of Building Space	3.0%	.4%	1.3%	0.0%	0.0%	0.0%	1.4%	2%	.6%
	(1)	(1)	(5)	(0)	(0)	(0)	(4)	(1)	(5)
Lack of Orders	.8%	0.0%	.3%	0.0%	0.0%	0.0%	.4%	0.0%	.1%
	(1)	(0)	(1)	(0)	(0)	(0)	(1)	(0)	(1)
Enhancement of Electricity Rates	0.0%	0.0%	0.0%	.7%	0.0%	.3%	.4%	0.0%	.1%
	(0)	(0)	(0)	(1)	(0)	(1)	(1)	(0)	(1)
Lack of Capital	27.1%	33.1%	31.1%	29.3%	31.9%	30.9%	28.2%	32.5%	31.0%
	(36)	(87)	(123)	(43)	(80)	(123)	(79)	(167)	(246)
Lack of Credit	20.3%	17.9%	18.7%	25.2%	18.3%	20.9%	22.9%	18.1%	19.8%
	(27	(47)	(74)	(37)	(46)	(83)	(64)	(93)	(157)
Lack of Managerial Skills	0.0%	.4%	.3%	1.4%	.4%	.8%	.7%	.4%	.5%
	(0)	(1)	(1)	(2)	(1)	(3)	(2)	(2)	(4)
Lack of Skilled Workers	5.3%	1.5%	2.8%	6.8%	8.4%	7.8%	6.1%	4.9%	5.3%
	(7)	(4)	(11)	(10)	(21)	(31)	(17)	(25)	(42)

Contd.

TABLE 3 (Contd.)

Urban, Informal Manufacturing
Distribution of Enterprises by Problems Being Faced at Present and By Type and Location of Units
All Manufacturing Activities

	City								
	Karachi			Gujranwala					
Problems Being Faced at Present	House Holds	Small Units	Total	House Holds	Small Units	Total	House Holds	Small Units	Total
High Turn-over of Workers	3.8%	3.4%	3.5%	2.7%	.8%	1.5%	3.2%	2.1%	2.5%
	(5)	(9)	(14)	(4)	(2)	(6)	(9)	(11)	(20)
Low Demand of Product	12.0%	8.7%	9.8%	10.9%	16.3%	14.3%	11.4%	12.5%	12.1%
	(16)	(23)	(39)	(16)	(41)	(57)	(32)	(64)	(96)
Competition from Similar	4.5%	10.6%	8.6%	4.8%	10.4%	8.3%	4.6%	10.5%	8.4%
Enterprises	(6)	(28)	(34)	(7)	(26)	(33)	(13)	(54)	(67)
Competition from Larger Enterprise	0.0%	6.1%	4.0%	.7%	1.2%	1.0%	.4%	3.7%	2.5%
	(0)	(16)	(16)	(1)	(3)	(4)	(1)	(19)	(20)
Insecurity/Riots	7.5%	7.6%	7.6%	1.4%	1.2%	1.3%	4.3%	4.5%	4.4%
	(10)	(20)	(30)	(2)	(3)	(5)	(12)	(23)	(35)
Loadshedding	2.3%	9.9%	7.3%	15.0%	11.2%	12.6%	8.9%	10.5%	9.9%
	(3)	(26)	(29)	(22)	(28)	(50)	(25)	(54)	(79)
Lack of Raw—Material	11.3%	0.0%	3.8%	1.4%	0.0%	.5%	6.1%	0.0%	2.1%
	(15)	(0)	(15)	(2)	(0)	(2)	(17)	(0)	(17)
Low Income	—	—	—	—	—	—	—	—	—

Number in Parenthesis.

Source: Project Urban Informal Manufacturing Survey, FBS 1990.

TABLE 4

Urban, Informal Manufacturing
Distribution of Sampled Workers Who Migrated by Reason for Migration, by Type and Location of Units
All Manufacturing Activites

	City								
	Karachi			Gujranwala					
Reason for Migration	House Hold	Small Unit	Column Total	House Hold	Small Unit	Column Total	House Hold	Small Unit	Column Total
No Work Available as Landless	23.5%	3.6%	6.3%	9.5%	12.5%	12.0%	15.8%	8.1%	9.2%
Labourer	(4)	(4)	(8)	(2)	(14)	(16)	(6)	(18)	(24)
No Work Available as Artisan	5.9%	.9%	1.6%	0.0%	6.3%	5.3%	2.6%	3.6%	3.4%
	(1)	(1)	(2)	(0)	(7)	(7)	(1)	(8)	(9)
Migrated With Family of Family	5.9%	31.5%	28.1%	23.8%	22.3%	22.6%	15.8%	26.9%	25.3%
Already Migrated	(1)	(35)	(36)	(5)	(25)	(30)	(6)	(60)	(66)
Expected Higher Income in City	52.9%	27.9%	31.3%	33.3%	39.3%	38.3%	42.1%	33.6%	34.9%
	(9)	(31)	(40)	(7)	(44)	(51)	(16)	(75)	(91)
Seeking Education and Skilling	0.0%	0.0%	0.0%	9.5%	2.7%	3.8%	5.3%	1.3%	1.9%
	(0)	(0)	(0)	(2)	(3)	(5)	(2)	(3)	(5)
Creation of Pakistan	11.8%	15.3%	14.8%	0.0%	8.9%	7.5%	5.3%	12.1%	11.1%
	(2)	(17)	(19)	(0)	(10)	(10)	(2)	(27)	(29)
Religious/Political Reasons	0.0%	19.8%	17.2%	9.5%	1.8%	3.0%	5.3%	10.8%	10.0%
	(0)	(22)	(22)	(2)	(2)	(4)	(2)	(24)	(26)
Domicile/ Marital Reasons	0.0%	0.0%	0.0%	4.8%	6.3%	6.0%	2.6%	3.1%	3.1%
	(0)	(0)	(0)	(1)	(7)	(8)	(1)	(7)	(8)
Other	0.0%	0.9%	0.8%	9.6%	0.0%	1.6%	5.2%	0.4%	1.2%
	(0)	(1)	(1)	(2)	(0)	(2)	(2)	(1)	(3)
Row Total	(17)	(111)	(128)	(21)	(112)	(133)	(38)	(223)	(261)
	13.3%	86.7%	100.0%	15.8%	84.2%	100.0%	14.6%	85.4%	100.0%

Source: Project Urban Informal Manufacturing Survey, FBS 1990.

Index

Abdul Aziz Anwar 37
Aftab, Khalid 97
Aggregate GDP growth 25
Agha Khan Rural Support Project 103
Agricultural Censuses 41-42, 54,60
—, of 1972 12
Agricultural Development Bank of Pakistan 11
Agricultural growth in Pakistan 2
Akmal Hussain 35, 60
Allama Iqbal Open University 104
Annual Establishment Enquiry 42-43
Annual Report on Contract Labour 43
Applied Economic Research Centre 36
Asian Regional Team for Employment Promotion 4

Bangladesh, creation of 2
Behbud NGO 103

Career development 80-81
Census of Manufacturing Industry 66
Changing demands for employment 25-28
Changing supply of people 24-25
Computer simulation 28-32
Contraceptive Prevalance Survey 107
Contract labour, Annual Report 43
Contract workers 81
—, (Tables) 66, 67
Crime Statistics (Table) 84

Data sources 43

Eckert, Jerry 34
Economic activity for women 101-107
Education, Sub-sectors (Table) 72
Education system of Pakistan 77
Emigration to Gulf region 16-18, 27-28
Employing units, small scale 84-91
Employment, changing demands 25-28
—, historical background 1-20
—, in agriculture 10-12
—, in urban sectors 15-16
—, strategy formulation 18-20
Employment creation 76-91
—, 1990's 21-39
Employment Exchanges 38
Employment generation 58-75, 92-108
—, in public sector 67-69
—, in small scale units 97-101
—, (Tables) 14
Employment performances, target 5-9
Employment units 74-75
Enrolment in education institutions 70

Factories Act 1934 43
Fareedy, Fareed Ahmad 42
Federal Bureau of Statistics 43, 57, 86,95
Female Labour Force Participation (Table) 52
Female Representation by Occupation (Table) 74
Five Year Plans 3-5, 7

Gallup (Pakistan) Ltd. 36
Green Revolution 6,19
Guisinger et al. 34, 35, 85

Hafeez Sabeeha 81, 82
Hira Shima 34
Household Incomes (Table) 9
Household level 76-79
Housing, Economic & Demographic Survey 8,41
Human Resource Development, historical background 1-20
—, strategy formulation 18-20
—, training for 95-97
Human Resource Skill Development 69-73

ILO-ARTEP 5
IMF 40
Import policy 2
Industrial Relations Ordinance 43
Industrialisation of Pakistan 2
Information requirement 94-95
Information system, Labour market 40-57
International labour emigration 27
International return migration 25
Investment Advisory Centre of Pakistan 4
Irfan M. 4, 5, 32, 34, 85

Jaffe, A.J. 44
Jameel Khan 34
Job preference (Table) 55
Job satisfaction (Table) 56

Karwanski 4
Kemal, A.R. 5, 31, 96
Khan, A. R. 34

Labour Absorption Changes (Table) 59
Labour emigration, Gulf region 16-18, 27-28
Labour exodus 17
Labour force measurement 47-56
Labour force participation rates 22, 24, 45, 56
(Tables) 46, 47, 48,49
Labour force pattern, in Pakistan 44
Labour Force Surveys 17, 42, 45, 60, 76
Labour market 21-24, 40-57
—, balances 28-32
—, feedbacks 32
—, imbalances 82-84
Labour Market Information System 40-57, 58, 94,
Labour migration in Gulf countries 79
Land distribution (Tables) 12
Large scale enterprises 100
Large scale investment 90
Lee, Mu Keun 96

Macro-economic impact of labour exodus 17
Macro-economic policy 58
Manpower planning 3-5
Manufacturing employment 13-15
Manufacturing Establishments (Table) 87
Manufacturing Industries, Census 42-43, 57, 66

Market forces 36,94,99
Maternity Benefit Ordinance 1958 43
Maxi Pak Wheat 10
Mehboob Elahi 34
Migration, rural-urban 32-33
Migration choice 79
Mines Act 1923 43
MInistry of Women Development 106
Moore, W.E. 44

Nadvi, Khalid M.97
Naseem, S.M. 35
National Commission on Agriculture 62,95
National Development Volunteer Programme 8
National Manpower Council 37
National Manpower Commission 19, 24,25, 27, 36, 38, 40, 43, 45, 59, 62, 66, 68, 71, 72, 74, 79, 91, 95, 96, 107

Occupational responses 33-34
Open educated unemployment 36-39
Orangi Pilot Project 103

Pakistan, development strategies 1-3
Pakistan economy 88
Paskistan Federal Bureau of Statistics 47
see also Federal Bureau of Statistics
Pakistani workers, in Gulf Region 8
Payment of Wages Act 1936 43
Peoples Works Programme 8
Planning Commission 95
Policy framework for employment generation 92-101
Population Censuses 41
Population growth 7
Poverty 38-39
Problems of unemployment 37
Provincial Labour Directorates 43,57
Public sector 67-69

Royal Commission Report 10
Rural employment, non-farm 12-13
Rural-rural migration 32-33
Rural Small Scale Industries (Table) 86
—, Survey (Tables) 115-157
Rural-urban migration 32-33
Rural Wages (Table) 89
Ruud, Kare 4

Sabolo's Economic Model 4

Semi-skilled Workers (Table) 71
Seventh Plan 93
Seventh Plan Policy Proposal 32
Shops & Establishment Ordinance 1959 43
Simulation Model Assumptions (Table) 23
Simulation Model Results (Tables) 28-31
Sixth Five Year Plan 10
Skilled Workers (Tables) 70-72
Small scale employing units 84-91
Small scale industries 98
Small Scale Industries Corporation 100
Small Scale Manufacturing (Table) 89
Small scale units 97-101
Stewart C.D. 44
Systems (Pvt.) Ltd. 42, 85

Training, need for 58-75
Training Institutions, Output (Table) 72
Turnhaume, D. 44

Unemployment, among educated manpower 37
Unemployment, open educated 36-39
Unemployment, (Tables) 50
Urban Small Scale Industries 86
—, Survey (Tables) 159-166
Urban wages (Table) 89

Wage Rate, Ratio (Table) 63
West Pakistan Industrial and Commercial Employment Standing Order Ordinance 1968 4
Wizarat, Shahida 63
Women Development Officer 106
'Women in Mainstream Development' 82
Women workers 81
Women's Development Bank 105
Women's employment and training 71
Women's labour force participation rates 48
Women's lack of choice 79-80
Women's polytechnics 104
World Bank 31

Zafar, Naeem ud Din 63

www.ingramcontent.com/pod-product-compliance
Ingram Content Group UK Ltd.
Pitfield, Milton Keynes, MK11 3LW, UK
UKHW041829200726
13854UKWH00002BA/895